More SCENES THAT HAPPEN

Real-life snapshots
of teenage lives

MARY KRELL-OISHI

Meriwether Publishing Ltd.
Colorado Springs, Colorado

Meriwether Publishing Ltd., Publisher
PO Box 7710
Colorado Springs, CO 80933-7710

Editor: Theodore O. Zapel
Cover design: Tom Myers

© Copyright MCMXCIV Meriwether Publishing Ltd.
Printed in the United States of America
First Edition

Library of Congress Cataloging-in-Publication Data

Krell-Oishi, Mary, 1953-
    More Scenes that happen : dramatized snapshots about the real life of high schoolers / by Mary Krell-Oishi -- 1st ed.
        p.   cm.
    ISBN-13: 978-1-56608-000-2
    ISBN-10: 1-56608-000-2
    1. High school students--Drama. 2. Young adult drama, American.
3. Acting. [1. High schools--Drama. 2. Schools--Drama. 3. Plays.] I. Title.
    PS3561.R425M6 1993
    812'.54--dc20   93-40926
                                                              CIP

4   5   6   07   08   09

To my sisters,
Kris and Janice,
For their love, friendship, inspiration and humor.

TABLE OF CONTENTS

BOYS

MIXED

NOTE: The numerals running vertically down the left margin of each page of dialog are for the convenience of the director. With these, he/she may easily direct attention to a specific passage.

The numerals in parentheses indicate number of persons in each play.

PREFACE

"I found a new book of scenes!" Because I am always in search of new material for my students, those are words that have always excited me during my career of teaching high school drama. However, my excitement was at times diminished, because of the quality or content of those scenes. Over the past few years, since the publication of my first book, I have had the joy of hearing words I wrote come from the mouths of wonderful young actors. I have had many drama teachers contact me at a festival or competition to tell me how much their students love doing the scenes that I wrote. Better yet, I have heard it from the students themselves.

Several times, while at one high school theatre festival or another, I have watched scenes that looked strangely familiar. Much to my pleasure and surprise, the scenes were mine. You can imagine my excitement to see the characters I have created being beautifully portrayed by a young actor who believes the words. What needs to be remembered by those of us who teach drama is that there are kids out there who can relate to being dumped in a relationship, being ignored by friends, or "cruising" the house of someone they admire for that stolen glimpse of a good-looking face. Not all kids are on drugs or in trouble with the law. Nor are most kids hoping to portray that on stage.

I must take this time to thank my fellow drama teachers, Gai Jones at El Dorado High School, Joe Parrish at Buena Park High School, and Ron Perry at Sunny Hills High School, for their unending support of the scenes I create. They have tried them out on their students and told me what works and what doesn't. Without their input from day one, encouraging me in my writing, not only would this book not exist, but I doubt that I would have had the courage to attempt publication of a first book.

This second book of scenes contains material more challenging in many degrees to those of the first book. However, my first concern remains the same: Believable characters who represent, honestly, high school students. It is my hope that you, too, find these characters accessible, honest and real, and that they are portrayed in that way. But most of all, have fun.

Mary Krell-Oishi

INTRODUCTION

Mary Krell-Oishi is a careful observer of the young people who surround her in her life as a high school teacher. She has taken advantage of her observations to write a wide variety of scenes that reflect the lives, attitudes and concerns of her students.

These scenes provide opportunities for young people to play roles that intersect with their own experience. Some of the scenes deal with serious issues, such as teenage pregnancy, peer pressure and young love, while others offer light-hearted looks at the everyday concerns of young people. Across the board, they celebrate the kind of friendship that makes adolescence bearable and memorable.

The scenes can be presented individually or put together into an evening of entertainment. They can be used as audition pieces or classroom exercises or to prompt discussion about specific issues. Or they can simply be performed for the sheer pleasure that comes from exploring theatrical possibilities. However they may be used, these scenes will provide pleasure, provoke thought and stimulate the imaginations of both performers and audiences.

> John Glore, Literary Manager of
> Tony Award-Winning South Coast
> Repertory, Costa Mesa, California,
> and author of the children's plays,
> *Wind of a Thousand Tales* and
> *Folktales Too.*

◆ GIRLS ◆

MISS PERFECT

TERI: Pretty, energetic, seems to have a lot going for her.

JAN: Teri's best friend. Not as excitable as Teri, more stable in her outlook.

SETTING: Scene takes place in JAN's house. The girls are studying, talking, just being friends.

JAN: I don't know how you do it.

TERI: Do what?

JAN: Balance it all. Cheerleading, grades, boys, everything. What did you get on that test in trig yesterday?

TERI: An A.

JAN: Of course.

TERI: Why, what did you get?

JAN: A C minus. And I was happy to see it. I *hate* trig. It is so stupid. Why do we have to take it?

TERI: So we can get into a good college.

JAN: Why do I bother? I am going to end up at the JC. Me and the rest of the morons.

TERI: Now, stop it.

JAN: I'm serious. I will end up in that intellectual vacuum, majoring in something really special, like say, typing. My life is hell. All because of *trig!*

TERI: Jan, all you have to do is apply yourself.

JAN: I do apply myself, "Mom." And thanks for the lecture.

TERI: I'm not lecturing you.

JAN: Geez, that's what it's beginning to sound like. If I want this, I'll go home.

TERI: You are home.

JAN: See what I mean? This stupid trig and all this other stuff has got me so messed up, I don't even know where I am.

TERI: Let's not get carried away, OK? Sit back down and I will help you, all right?

1   **JAN:**   **It's a lost cause. I'm a lost cause. Math is a lost cause.**
2   **TERI:**   **So, you're just going to give up.**
3   **JAN:**   **Only for a moment.** **Just long enough to eat something**
4   **very, very rich and very, very nasty. Something**
5   **completely off any diet ever conceived.** *(She crosses to the*
6   *fridge.)* **Let's see what we have here.** *(She begins to pull food*
7   *out.)* **How about this cake, and some milk . . . ooohhh, look,**
8   **here's some cookie dough Mom made last night.** *(She pulls*
9   *out a few other things and spreads them on the table.)* **Help**
10   **yourself.**
11   **TERI:**   **Do you have any apples?**
12   **JAN:**   **I offer you the food of the gods, chocolate chip cookie**
13   **dough made fresh last night, and you want an apple?**
14   **TERI:**   **Some of us care about how we look, Jan.**
15   **JAN:**   **I care, Teri. Just not right now. And what are you**
16   **worried about? You are as thin as a rail.**
17   **TERI:**   **That's because I watch what I eat, I exercise, and I am**
18   **careful about my body.**
19   **JAN:**   **Like I care, right?** *(She takes a spoonful of cookie dough.)*
20   **It's good stuff, Teri.**
21   **TERI:**   **Well, maybe a bite.**
22   **JAN:**   **That's what I like to see.**
23   **TERI:**   *(TERI proceeds to eat throughout the rest of the scene unless*
24   *otherwise noted.)* **This is good, isn't it?**
25   **JAN:**   **I told you.**
26   **TERI:**   **Well, as long as I'm careful. I wouldn't want to end up**
27   **looking like Marlene.**
28   **JAN:**   **That cow? Never, not you.**
29   **TERI:**   **Well, you can't be too careful, you know.**
30   **JAN:**   **You need to loosen up, Teri, you know that? You are**
31   **wound tighter than a watch spring.**
32   **TERI:**   **What?**
33   **JAN:**   **You are so intense. You do everything at school, you**
34   **are your mommy and daddy's perfect little girl with your**
35   **stupid 4.0, David worships the ground you float over, and**

1   to add insult to injury, you're a cheerleader. If I weren't
2   your best friend, I think I would hate your guts.
3   TERI: Gee, thanks.
4   JAN: I'm serious. How do you do it all?
5   TERI: I just do it, I guess. It's no big deal. *(She starts in on the*
6   *cake, perhaps putting it in a bowl and pouring the milk over it.)*
7   JAN: *(Watching this)* Well, at least you have disgusting eating
8   habits. What the hell are you doing?
9   TERI: Eating cake and milk.
10   JAN: You ate almost all of that cookie dough, and now you're
11   going to start in on cake? I thought I ate a lot.
12   TERI: I guess I'm just hungry. I haven't eaten all day.
13   JAN: Yes, you did. You had three hot dogs and finished
14   David's hamburger at lunch.
15   TERI: Oh, yeah. I forgot.
16   JAN: I swear, you eat a lot. Where do you put it all?
17   TERI: *(Her mouth full)* Hmmm?
18   JAN: You are so skinny. I wish I could eat like you and not
19   gain weight. I just look at Haagen-Dazs and I gain five
20   pounds.
21   TERI: I'm just lucky, I guess.
22   JAN: I guess. *(She starts to put the cake away.)*
23   TERI: Hey, there's not that much there. I'll finish it up, OK?
24   JAN: Fine. *(She watches her plow away the food for a moment.)* I
25   really don't get it.
26   TERI: Stop watching me. It makes me nervous.
27   JAN: Sorry. *(She clears the cookie dough bowl away.)* You want
28   anything else?
29   TERI: What have you got?
30   JAN: Teri, I was kidding.
31   TERI: Oh.
32   JAN: *Do* you want anything?
33   TERI: No. Really. I'm fine.
34   JAN: OK. You gonna help me with this stupid trig now?
35   TERI: Sure. Sit down.

1   **JAN: OK. Let's get started.**

2   **TERI: Oh.** *(They get papers and book ready.)* **Wait a minute. I**

3   **need to use the bathroom.**

4   **JAN: Everyone would be shocked to know what Miss Perfect**

5   **does, huh?**

6   **TERI: Does what?**

7   **JAN: Tinkles.**

8   **TERI: Oh, stop it. I'll be back in a minute.**

9   **JAN: Sure. I'll just clean up your cake soup.** *(TERI exits and*

10   *JAN puts the bowl in the sink.)* **This is really disgusting,**

11   **Teri.** *(She sits back down, picks up the book and tries to go over*

12   *the math work.)* **OK, if I take this and add that, then it is . . .**

13   *(She figures for a minute, and then checks her answer with*

14   *TERI's work.)* ***Still wrong! Argh!***

15   **TERI: What now?**

16   **JAN: *I hate math!***

17   **TERI: Let's see if I can help you. OK.** *(She looks over JAN's*

18   *work.)* **Well, dummy, here's your problem.** *(As she picks up*

19   *the pencil, she drops it. She is a little shaky.)* **Ooops.**

20   **JAN: Teri, are you all right?** *(She looks closely at her.)* **Teri, you**

21   **look sick.**

22   **TERI: I'm fine. Honest. Just a little shaky.**

23   **JAN: You know, you've been shaky a lot lately.**

24   **TERI: Have I?**

25   **JAN: Yeah, now that I think about it. You also have these**

26   **circles under your eyes.**

27   **TERI: I've just been tired lately, because of all the stuff I'm**

28   **doing.**

29   **JAN: Are you sure?**

30   **TERI: Jan, I'm fine. Don't worry about it.**

31   **JAN: But I do worry. What's going on with you?**

32   **TERI: Nothing. Let's just get to work, OK?**

33   **JAN: No, it's not OK. I want to know what's going on.**

34   **TERI: If you must know, I was sick just now. Sometimes, it**

35   **makes me a little weak.**

1	JAN:	What do you mean sometimes? What do you mean sick?
2	TERI:	Sick, you know, sick. Praying to the porcelain god,
3		worshiping Ralph, all the metaphors.
4	JAN:	Why? Do you have the flu or something?
5	TERI:	Jan, I am going to let you in on a little secret. You want
6		to know how I can eat anything and not gain weight? I'll
7		tell you. I just throw up what I eat.
8	JAN:	What?
9	TERI:	It's no big deal. I don't do it all the time. Just when I
10		eat too much, like just now. That way, I don't deny myself,
11		I eat what I want, and I don't gain weight.
12	JAN:	Teri, that's called bulimia.
13	TERI:	Only if you do it all the time. I don't.
14	JAN:	That's twice today, isn't it?
15	TERI:	What do you mean?
16	JAN:	After you ate everybody's food at lunch, you left for a
17		while. When you came back, you were shaky then, too.
18	TERI:	Today was a lot. I eat when I'm nervous. And lately I
19		have a ton of stuff to be nervous about.
20	JAN:	Teri, you shouldn't do that.
21	TERI:	And you say I'm tense. Lighten up. I'm fine.
22	JAN:	You do this all the time, don't you?
23	TERI:	No, not all the time. Just enough to make sure I don't
24		gain weight.
25	JAN:	This is unbelievable.
26	TERI:	What? That perfect Teri isn't so perfect? That Little
27		Miss Wonderful has to work a little harder than everyone
28		else to stay thin?
29	JAN:	No, that you think it matters so much that you'd risk
30		your health to do it.
31	TERI:	So, call the care unit.
32	JAN:	You need help with this problem.
33	TERI:	There is no *problem*. I know what I'm doing. I can
34		stop anytime I want.
35	JAN:	Then stop now.

1   TERI: I said when I want, not when you want me to.
2   JAN: This is sick. This is wrong. You could cause a lot of
3   problems for yourself.
4   TERI: Dammit, Jan, who made you God? I handle my life my
5   way. Who's the one with the grades, the boyfriend, the
6   size four clothes, the adoring parents, the head
7   cheerleader? Who? Not you, that's for damn sure.
8   JAN: Who's the one throwing up every day?
9   TERI: If I want to stay like this, I have to. I have to be in
10   control of this.
11   JAN: You're not in control. You're out of control.
12   TERI: You don't know what you're talking about. I have a
13   handle on everything. I'm perfect, just like everyone
14   expects me to be. I can't let anyone down.
15   JAN: What about you?
16   TERI: I take care of me. I do everything everyone expects
17   of me. I make sure that no one is disappointed. Looking
18   good is the one thing I do for me.
19   JAN: At the risk of your health?
20   TERI: Back off, Jan.
21   JAN: No, I will not. This is so wrong, so bad. I can't believe
22   you are being so stupid. No one would love you less if
23   you weren't skinny.
24   TERI: *(Over JAN's speaking)* Shut up, shut up, shut up, just
25   shut up. You don't understand.
26   JAN: Help me to.
27   TERI: Everyone expects me to be this, I don't know, this
28   little model of perfection. You know, my dad still stops
29   everything, wherever we are and sings "There She Is,
30   Miss America" whenever I walk into a room. Even at the
31   store. And David, he walks me around at school like I'm
32   his personal arm decoration. One more thing . . . have you
33   ever seen a fat cheerleader?
34   JAN: Teri, you're exaggerating . . .
35   TERI: *(Beginning to get angry again)* No, Jan, I'm not.

1   **JAN:**   You've got to get some help.

2   **TERI:**   *(Getting angrier)* **Just leave me alone about it, OK?**

3   **JAN:**   **No, I can't. I think you need to tell your parents what is**

4   **going on.**

5   **TERI:**   *(Starting to flip out, the rest of the dialog is very quick until*

6   *the last line.)* **No! Just leave me alone, dammit, leave me**

7   **alone. I shouldn't have told you, and I am not telling my**

8   **parents anything.**

9   **JAN:**   **Teri, you have to.**

10   **TERI:**   **Absolutely not. This is the one thing in my life I have**

11   **total control over. Just leave me alone about it.**

12   **JAN:**   **But Teri, you're going to end up dead if you keep this up.**

13   **TERI:**   **I'd rather be dead than fat.** *(She glares at JAN, and then*

14   *exits.)*

15

16

17

18

19

20

21

22

23

24

25

26

27

28

29

30

31

32

33

34

35

UNRESOLVED CONFLICT

3 *CASSIE:* Recovering from a serious illness, self-absorbed.
4 *LINDA:* Her devoted but exhausted friend, image conscious.
5 *SETTING:* Bare stage, two chairs.
6
7 **LINDA:** **Hi.**
8 **CASSIE:** **Hi.** *(They both sit quietly for a moment, uncomfortably.)*
9 **LINDA:** **Are you going to talk to me?**
10 **CASSIE:** **What about?**
11 **LINDA:** **Anything. Everything.**
12 **CASSIE:** **There's nothing really to say, is there?**
13 **LINDA:** **Cassie, I am really sorry. I am.**
14 **CASSIE:** **Well, you say that, but I don't think I can believe you.**
15 **LINDA:** **I didn't know you wanted to ask Joey to the dance.**
16   **I didn't.**
17 **CASSIE:** **Oh, please. You knew I liked him, but you couldn't**
18   **wait to snap him up, could you?**
19 **LINDA:** **If you are going to be this upset by it, I will call him**
20   **right now and un-ask him.**
21 **CASSIE:** **Do what you want. You always do.**
22 **LINDA:** **That's unfair, Cassie.**
23 **CASSIE:** **Is it? Lately it seems as though you have to be**
24   **number one, not only in your life, but in everyone else's.**
25   **Well, face it, Linda, the world does not revolve around**
26   **you.**
27 **LINDA:** **I never said it did.**
28 **CASSIE:** **No, you just act like it. You take everything, and**
29   **make sure that you're the center of it. You're only around**
30   **if it makes you look good.**
31 **LINDA:** **I am always there for you . . . through everything.**
32 **CASSIE:** **I know you'd like to think so, but you're wrong.**
33 **LINDA:** **When haven't I been there for you? Who stood by**
34   **your side when you were sick? It sure as hell wasn't**
35   **Leanna or Rebecca. It was me.**

10

1 CASSIE: I'm over the physical problems I had. Now I need
2   you to be there as a friend. Just a friend.
3 LINDA: I am. I have been.
4 CASSIE: A real friend doesn't sneak around behind your
5   back. A real friend talks to you, not about you.
6 LINDA: I have never talked about you.
7 CASSIE: Come off it, Lin. I have been the focus of your after-
8   school conversation for months now . . .
9 LINDA: Wrong! People have been concerned about you, so
10   they ask me how you are and . . .
11 CASSIE: They can ask me . . .
12 LINDA: The hell they can. No one can talk to you. No one can
13   get near you. You have closed yourself off totally from me.
14 CASSIE: Can you blame me? I can't believe that I
15   trusted you . . .
16 LINDA: I honestly didn't know you liked Joey . . .
17 CASSIE: This isn't about Joey, dammit. I can't believe you
18   think I would be this upset about some guy.
19 LINDA: Then what? Explain it to me.
20 CASSIE: Leanna told me what you said.
21 LINDA: What? What did she tell you?
22 CASSIE: That you were sick of how hard it is to be my friend.
23   Well, I guess you really proved that, because a real friend
24   doesn't do the things you've done.
25 LINDA: What horrible things have I done? Yes, I said it's hard
26   to be your friend. Face it, Cassie, it has been. You were
27   so sick for so long. It was exhausting for me.
28 CASSIE: Well, it wasn't exactly a walk in the park for me.
29 LINDA: I know that. But, dammit, you drained me. So, yes, I
30   said I was tired of you being so sick. We all were.
31 CASSIE: Well, thanks a lot. Next time I'll try to die so you
32   won't have to be put out.
33 LINDA: Don't be an idiot.
34 CASSIE: Don't call me an idiot. You act like my illness was a
35   burden for you. Well, I'm sorry, but it happened. And now

1   it's over.

2   LINDA: Is it? Every time you get tired, we all get scared. We

3   don't know what's going to happen. You don't know what

4   it's like watching you slowly fade away right in front of

5   us, and there is nothing we can do.

6   CASSIE: How do you think I feel?

7   LINDA: I haven't the faintest idea any more. You totally shut

8   us all out.

9   CASSIE: I'm just tired of dealing with it. With the sickness,

10   with the feelings, with everything.

11   LINDA: Well, then, can you blame us?

12   CASSIE: Not the rest of them, but I can blame you. You were

13   supposed to be there for me, through everything.

14   LINDA: I have been . . .

15   CASSIE: No, you're there to soak up the feelings. Sometimes

16   I felt like you just wanted to be around me so people

17   would say, "Wow, what a good friend Linda is to Cassie.

18   Look at her." And you could walk around with that little

19   sad face and everyone would ask you what's wrong. And

20   you could tell them about how strong you have to be for

21   poor pathetic Cassie.

22   LINDA: That's ridiculous.

23   CASSIE: Is it? I don't think so. There have been times when

24   I watch you right after you hug me and I can see your

25   eyes darting around, making sure that people see you

26   being supportive of me. It's like this little game of glory

27   for you, isn't it?

28   LINDA: Where is all of this coming from? I have been the best

29   friend you could have.

30   CASSIE: You'd like to believe that, wouldn't you? *(Getting up*

31   *and leaving)* Well, you may have been, but you're not now.

32   LINDA: What are you talking about? What is the problem?

33   CASSIE: I don't know. I just know that I thought you were

34   my friend. And this thing with Joey, small though it is,

35   just points out that you don't think about anyone but

1   yourself.

2   LINDA: So you're just going to turn your back on me and

3   leave?

4   CASSIE: I think you turned your back on me a long time ago.

5   LINDA: *(Completely confused)* **What?**

6   CASSIE: Don't act stupid, Linda.

7   LINDA: Honestly, I don't know what you want from me.

8   CASSIE: I want honesty. I want total honesty from you. I

9   thought that's what friendship was based on, but I guess

10   you don't feel the same way.

11   LINDA: I have been honest. And I've been there for you,

12   through all the crap you've been through.

13   CASSIE: No, Linda, that's how it used to be. If you really were

14   there for me, you would have known that I liked Joey

15   and you would have taken my feelings into consideration.

16   LINDA: This is about more than just Joey. If you have some-

17   thing to say, you just better say it. I don't have time for

18   these stupid games.

19   CASSIE: No, you don't have time for me. Or my feelings. Or

20   my pain. You know what I've been through. You were

21   there, and I thought you'd always be there for me. But I

22   was wrong. You took my trust and used it so you could

23   look good by being my friend.

24   LINDA: It always comes down to this, doesn't it? It's always

25   about you.

26   CASSIE: I'm the one who was wronged here.

27   LINDA: You know what, you can just go to hell.

28   CASSIE: Excuse me?

29   LINDA: You heard me. You can go to hell. I have had it up to

30   here with you and your feelings. You have become the

31   most self-centered, self-absorbed person I know. This

32   isn't about Joey. This is about you . . . as usual. I spent

33   the whole summer with you, worried about you, hovering

34   over your hospital bed, not knowing whether you were

35   going to live or die. You're damn right I walk around with

1   a sad face. But it's certainly not to get sympathy. You do
2   that well enough for both of us. Hell, you do it well enough
3   for everyone.
4   CASSIE: I don't need your pity. I don't need anybody's pity.
5   My life has been tough enough for long enough and I am
6   sick of putting how I really feel on hold. My parents, my
7   brother, my sister, they all walk around like they don't
8   know what to say to me . . . so they just don't talk to me.
9   You have no idea what it's like to be so close to death
10   and have to face it alone.
11   LINDA: Alone? You were never alone. All of us — including
12   your family — were by your side the whole time.
13   CASSIE: I know that. But I still had to face it alone.
14   LINDA: Oh, yeah, your life is so rotten. No one cares enough
15   about poor little Cassie.
16   CASSIE: I'm leaving.
17   LINDA: Typical. So very typical of you. The minute you are
18   faced with any kind of real confrontation, you walk away.
19   Hell, you run away. You either get sick or walk out or
20   hide, but one way or another, you just don't deal, do you?
21   CASSIE: You don't know what you're talking about.
22   LINDA: Don't I? Take a look at your wrists, Cassie. You know
23   what I find interesting? Whenever you're upset, you wear
24   short sleeves and bracelets. Talk about calling attention
25   to something.
26   CASSIE: Bull.
27   LINDA: You think? Look at what you've got on. Short sleeves
28   and bracelets. You're mad at me, so this way you come
29   in with your wounded body and I'm supposed to lay down
30   and give in.
31   CASSIE: You're a riot. You should be a psychologist.
32   LINDA: No, you need to see one.
33   CASSIE: You are so full of it.
34   LINDA: You said you wanted honesty from me, well fine.
35   That's what you are going to get.

1   CASSIE: This isn't honesty.
2   LINDA: Yes, it is. You just can't deal with me being honest
3   with you because no one has been for so long. It's been,
4   "Oh, don't upset Cassie," or "Cassie's not well today, so
5   let's just do what she wants." Well, guess what? The world
6   does not revolve around Cassie Reynolds, hard though
7   that may be for you to believe.
8   CASSIE: I can't believe you would say that. I have never felt
9   that way.
10   LINDA: Oh, please. That's your basic M.O.
11   CASSIE: Well, then, I would say that you are exactly the same
12   way.
13   LINDA: Again, oh, please.
14   CASSIE: You know what I found out that was really
15   disgusting to me the last time I got out of the hospital?
16   I had so many people call me and tell me how hard you
17   were taking my being sick. Everyone was telling me how
18   they were so worried about *you* because you were so
19   upset. You weren't eating or sleeping because you were
20   so worried.
21   LINDA: Well, it was true.
22   CASSIE: *I was the sick one, dammit!* Not you. This was not
23   about you. It was about me ...
24   LINDA: Everything's about you, isn't it ...?
25   CASSIE: Unfair! That is completely unfair to say ...
26   LINDA: Is it? The whole school was talking about you, and
27   you loved it ...
28   CASSIE: I didn't. But you couldn't stand it, could you? You
29   had to be right there with the up-to-the-minute reports
30   for everyone.
31   LINDA: Don't be stupid.
32   CASSIE: *Don't call me stupid!*
33   LINDA: I will if that's how you're acting. And you're acting
34   stupid!
35   CASSIE: Sometimes I really hate you.

1 LINDA: Well, surprise, because sometimes I really hate you.
2 CASSIE: This always happens. People you trust just betray
3   you.
4 LINDA: Oh, come on. Don't throw that crap at me, because
5   I'm not falling into that trap.
6 CASSIE: Trap?
7 LINDA: Yes, trap. You always do this. The minute things go
8   against you, it's the guilt trap. Well, it's not working this
9   time. In fact, it's not working at all. And you know what?
10   I'm *not* calling Joey up and un-asking him to the dance.
11   If you wanted to ask him, you should have. You snooze,
12   you lose. And next time you fall off the health wagon,
13   don't expect me to come running to pick you up. I'm tired
14   of putting my life on hold to make sure that your life goes
15   well.
16 CASSIE: No one ever asked you to put your life on hold.
17 LINDA: Oh, I guess that was someone else calling me at all
18   hours of the day and night to spill their guts.
19 CASSIE: See! This is exactly why I have been closing myself
20   off from you. You don't want to hear about how I feel.
21 LINDA: Yes, I do. But I would like to hear some good stuff
22   about how you feel once in awhile.
23 CASSIE: There isn't any!
24 LINDA: Oh, yeah, your life is so hard.
25 CASSIE: You're a bitch.
26 LINDA: I learned from the best.
27 CASSIE: *(After a moment of silence)* What's happening here?
28 LINDA: Hey, you said you wanted honesty. Well, you got it.
29 CASSIE: I wanted my best friend.
30 LINDA: And how does one qualify for that post?
31 CASSIE: Certainly not the way you've been. Not by being so
32   selfish.
33 LINDA: You know, maybe you're right. Maybe I did feel kind
34   of good being the best friend of the sick girl. But, you
35   know, the tradeoff wasn't worth it. We had what I thought

1 was a great friendship. But maybe neither of us were
2 strong enough to stick it out for each other. I don't know.
3 All I know is that I am emotionally drained. The well is
4 empty.
5 CASSIE: Mine's been dry for a long time. I'm just too
6 exhausted to put forth the effort for anything, let alone
7 friendship.
8 LINDA: So, where does this leave us?
9 CASSIE: Alone?
10 LINDA: Are we still fighting?
11 CASSIE: No. If we were fighting, one of us would be wrong
12 and one of us would be right. I think this is what's called
13 "unresolved conflict."
14 LINDA: No winners, no losers.
15 CASSIE: No losers? I don't know about that.
16 LINDA: So, we just end.
17 CASSIE: You said some terrible things to me.
18 LINDA: So did you.
19 CASSIE: Do you take them back . . .?
20 LINDA: . . . No, I don't think I do.
21 CASSIE: . . . I don't either.
22 LINDA: So, we are unresolved. Are we still friends?
23 CASSIE: Not like we used to be.
24 LINDA: Maybe that's for the best.
25 CASSIE: And maybe it's not.
26 LINDA: Maybe . . .
27 CASSIE: Yeah, maybe . . .
28 LINDA: Sooo. I gotta go.
29 CASSIE: Me too.
30 LINDA: I'm really tired . . .
31 CASSIE: *(At the same time as LINDA)* **I'm exhausted** . . .
32 LINDA: *(She begins to exit.)* **See ya, Cass.**
33 CASSIE: **Hey!** *(LINDA turns.)* **Nothing.** *(LINDA nods, smiles*
34 *sadly, and leaves. CASSIE is alone. Quietly)* **See ya** . . .
35

1   # WINGS

2

3   *JESSICA:*   Average eighteen-year-old student.

4   *JERUSHA:*   Her sixteen-year-old sister, very cute, bright and active.

5   *SETTING:*   Family room.

6

7   **JESSICA: Jerusha, sit down, we need to talk.**

8   **JERUSHA: Can you make it fast? I've got a ton of stuff to do**

9   **and I'm running late.**

10   **JESSICA:** *(After a moment)* **Forget it. It's not important.** *(Begins*

11   *to exit.)* **You know, yes, it is important.**

12   **JERUSHA: Go ahead, what is it?**

13   **JESSICA: Do you think you could sit down long enough to**

14   **look at me in the eyes? Do you think that maybe you**

15   **could find a few minutes for your sister in your ever so**

16   **busy schedule?**

17   **JERUSHA: Jessica, you know I have to get to school early**

18   **to help set up for the pep rally.**

19   **JESSICA: And we all know how important that is, don't we?**

20   **JERUSHA: Listen, I know you're upset about something.**

21   **Instead of playing silly games, why don't you just tell me?**

22   **JESSICA: As soon as I am sure I have your attention, I will.**

23   **JERUSHA:** *(Sitting down, annoyed)* **OK, here I am. You have**

24   **my undivided attention.**

25   **JESSICA: Well, it's a first.**

26   **JERUSHA: If you don't just come out and say what's on your**

27   **mind, I'm going to get mad.**

28   **JESSICA: Wow. That will just destroy my day.**

29   **JERUSHA:** *(Getting up)* **I don't have time for your stupidity.**

30   **You have been an absolute rag for weeks, and I am sick**

31   **of it. You want to talk, catch me after school.**

32   **JESSICA:** *(Grabbing her)* **You'll talk to me now.**

33   **JERUSHA:** *(Pulling away)* **I have been trying to talk with you**

34   **for the last few minutes, but you're the one who won't**

35   **get to the point.**

1   JESSICA: That. That right there is my point.

2   JERUSHA: What?

3   JESSICA: Talking with. You never talk with me. Oh, you'll
4   talk around me, at me, to me, sometimes about me, but
5   you never talk *with* me.

6   JERUSHA: What does that mean?

7   JESSICA: It means that for the last few months, you have
8   become so completely self-absorbed that you don't even
9   realize there are other people around you. It's always
10   "me, me, me."

11   JERUSHA: You don't know what you're talking about.

12   JESSICA: Oh? Well, let me tell you something else. There are
13   other people in this world besides you.

14   JERUSHA: Jessica, get to the point.

15   JESSICA: The point is that I am tired of being the one who
16   does everything for everyone. Especially for you. I am
17   tired of carting you and your little loser friends
18   everywhere. I am tired of finding my clothes in your
19   closet. I am tired of hearing from everyone how cute you
20   are. If one more person tells me what a doll my sister is,
21   I think I will puke on their feet.

22   JERUSHA: Wait a minute. It's not my fault that people think
23   I'm cute. And I hate that word. You know I do.

24   JESSICA: Please, Jerusha, you love that word. You live to
25   have people tell you how adorable you are. How do you
26   think it makes me feel to have everyone always telling
27   me that my little sister is so cute and adorable and smart
28   and talented?

29   JERUSHA: I would hope the same way it makes me feel when
30   people tell me the same thing about you.

31   JESSICA: Give me a break. I am many things, but cute has
32   never been one of them.

33   JERUSHA: No. They don't say cute. They say beautiful.
34   Lovely. They also say talented and smart. And I am proud
35   when they say it because you're my big sister and I love you.

1   JESSICA: Don't hand me your usual line of people-pleasing
2   crap, if you don't mind.
3   JERUSHA: *(Getting angry)* And stop saying that. I hate it
4   when you say that.
5   JESSICA: It's true. You'll say and do anything to make
6   people happy and make them like you. It's sick. It's almost
7   sociopathic. You should seek psychiatric care for that,
8   you know?
9   JERUSHA: You're just jealous.
10   JESSICA: You know . . . I don't care enough about you
11   anymore for your insults to bother me. I just don't care
12   about you at all. You're not worth my time or my emotions.
13   JERUSHA: *(Looking at her, wide-eyed)* You don't mean that.
14   JESSICA: *(Very calmly)* Yes. Yes, I do.
15   JERUSHA: *(Crying)* No, you don't.
16   JESSICA: And your stupid tears don't get to me, either.
17   *(Beginning to feel badly)* Stop it. Just stop that fake crying.
18   JERUSHA: You are my only sister. I look up to you and try so
19   hard to make you not be mad at me. But you are always
20   mad at me, no matter what I do.
21   JESSICA: Stop it, Rush. *(Beginning to crumble)* Stop it. God, I
22   hate you. *(They are both crying now, looking at each other.)*
23   JERUSHA: Do you really?
24   JESSICA: *(Crying)* Yes . . . *(Looks at JERUSHA.)* No, no I don't
25   hate you. *(They fall into each other's arms.)* I just get so
26   jealous of you.
27   JERUSHA: Why? What do I do?
28   JESSICA: You are just you. Cute, and adored by everyone.
29   Straight A's. Cheerleader. Everything. It's hard having a
30   sister like you.
31   JERUSHA: I don't understand you. You are so talented and
32   beautiful . . .
33   JESSICA: Yeah, right . . .
34   JERUSHA: I hate when you do that. You are absolutely
35   beautiful. I wish you would just believe me. Maybe if you

1   believed in yourself as much as I do, you'd be happier.
2   JESSICA: I don't know how I'd be happier. I wish I were more
3   like you.
4   JERUSHA: No, you don't. You are the perfect you. I could
5   never have picked a better sister.
6   JESSICA: Yeah, you could have.
7   JERUSHA: No. You are the only sister I would want. I wish
8   I could be like you.
9   JESSICA: Yeah, right.
10   JERUSHA: I do. You are so contained.
11   JESSICA: Like canned beans? Thanks.
12   JERUSHA: No, idiot. Like a real adult person. You don't
13   worry about pleasing everyone. You are true to yourself.
14   Sometimes, I don't even know who I am.
15   JESSICA: I know who I am. Jerusha's big sister.
16   JERUSHA: Not even. There's so much more to you than just
17   that. You are yourself. Not the cheerleader, not the brain,
18   not any label. Just Jessica. Pure and perfect.
19   JESSICA: Sounds empty. That's how I feel.
20   JERUSHA: You shouldn't. You are unique. You're special.
21   And you bring me down to earth. You keep me honest.
22   JESSICA: I do? How?
23   JERUSHA: You let me know when I get to be "too much."
24   JESSICA: Which is a lot of the time. You know, though, you
25   make me see myself differently. Sometimes I don't know
26   if I like what I see. Like now. I'm sorry I said the things
27   I did.
28   JERUSHA: It's OK.
29   JESSICA: No, it's not. I'm a rotten sister. You should admit it.
30   Stop trying to be so nice. I said terrible things to you.
31   JERUSHA: But I need to hear them. I do get stupid
32   sometimes. But you set me straight. We are perfect for
33   each other.
34
35   *(DIRECTOR'S NOTE: If you have two girls who can sing, adding*

21

1   *the following is a really nice touch:)*
2 **JERUSHA:** **We are the wind beneath each other's wings.**
3   *(Begin singing song "Wind Beneath My Wings." JERUSHA*
4   *starts, JESSICA comes in after first line. Switch words to show*
5   *each is the other's hero.)*
6
7
8
9
10
11
12
13
14
15
16
17
18
19
20
21
22
23
24
25
26
27
28
29
30
31
32
33
34
35

BEST FRIENDS

CARA: In love with David, her boyfriend, and happy about her life.

KATE: Is not so terribly happy about her life, misses the companionship of her best friend.

SETTING: CARA and KATE are in the middle of a conversation. CARA is excited about her news. KATE listens absentmindedly, perhaps pulling on a thread of her sweater.

CARA: So, anyway, David told me that after the dance on Saturday, we are going to go out for a special midnight supper he has all planned.

KATE: *(Not showing all that much interest)* Oh, really?

CARA: Apparently he's been planning this for a while. You know what?

KATE: What, Cara?

CARA: I think he is going to ask me to be his girlfriend.

KATE: Isn't that what you already are?

CARA: No, not really. I mean, I don't see anyone else but him ...

KATE: No kidding.

CARA: What?

KATE: Nothing.

CARA: Oh. Anyway, I don't see anyone else but him, and I don't know if he does or not. See anyone else, I mean.

KATE: *(Sarcastic)* Oh, I'm sure he doesn't.

CARA: Well, at least, not anymore.

KATE: *(Still a bit sarcastic)* No, not anymore.

CARA: Kate, I know what you're hinting at. Him and that tramp, Rachel. Well, that was a long time ago ...

KATE: Yeah, at least a month.

CARA: ... And he is not seeing *anyone* but me now.

KATE: And you are not seeing *anyone* but him.

CARA: Why does that bother you so much?

KATE: It doesn't *bother* me. It just, you know, bugs.

CARA: Well, I'm sorry, but get past it. David and I are going

1   to be together, and that is that.

2 KATE: So, if he asks you to be exclusive, you're going to say
3   yes.

4 CARA: Absolutely.

5 KATE: Cara ... you want me to be honest with you, don't
6   you?

7 CARA: *(Looking at her for a moment)* Yes, of course I do.

8 KATE: Then I can't keep this a secret, especially if you are
9   deciding that you and David are going to be "married."

10 CARA: We're not married, we are going together.

11 KATE: With you, it's the same thing. You spend every
12   moment of your life with the guy you are going out with.
13   You might as well be married. Which is why I have to be
14   honest with you.

15 CARA: I don't want to hear anything against David.

16 KATE: Well, you're going to.

17 CARA: *No!*

18 KATE: Cara, listen to me. David came on to me. To me. Your
19   best friend.

20 CARA: When?

21 KATE: Remember the party at Kim's house? When you were
22   grounded? That night I was supposed to get a ride from
23   there with Chris, but she left with that Jimmy guy she
24   just met. Anyway, I didn't have a ride, so David gave me
25   one.

26 CARA: Yes?

27 KATE: *(Watching for CARA's reaction)* So, I got in the car with
28   him. We were just sitting there in front of my house,
29   talking. And then one thing led to another.

30 CARA: Uh-huh ...

31 KATE: Honestly, as soon as he kissed me, I pushed him away.

32 CARA: Did you?

33 KATE: Of course. We're best friends. I care about you, even if
34   David doesn't.

35 CARA: Why are you telling me this?

1	KATE: Cara, I have to. It's been eating me up inside. And
2	now, when you tell me that you are going to be "steady"
3	with only him, it turns my stomach.
4	CARA: You know, I was wondering if you would ever bring
5	this up.
6	KATE: If I would bring what up?
7	CARA: That night, what happened between you.
8	KATE: What? Did someone else tell you?
9	CARA: Yes. David did.
10	KATE: David? When? What did he say?
11	CARA: He called me that night. He told me that you came on
12	to him. He told me that at the party, you were hanging
13	all over him . . .
14	KATE: Oh, I'm sure he just wanted to cover his butt . . .
15	CARA: Kate, he called me from the party. He said that he
16	needed to talk to me because you were acting so weird
17	that night. He was afraid you had been drinking too
18	much. In fact, I was the one who told him to take you
19	home. He didn't want to.
20	KATE: Oh, yeah, right. He begged me to let him take me
21	home.
22	CARA: That's because I asked him to. We were both worried
23	about you, fools that we are.
24	KATE: Cara, you can't be serious that you really believe I
25	came on to him. I don't even like the guy.
26	CARA: Then why did you try to kiss him?
27	KATE: Me? I told you, he tried to kiss me. In fact, I was
28	getting a little scared. He got kind of rough.
29	CARA: Kate, he *called* me right when he got home. He
30	thought for sure you would tell him that he was the one.
31	And for a tiny little moment, I thought, yeah, maybe he
32	is covering all his bases. But then I thought, no. It's you.
33	You haven't liked David from the start and I think you
34	would do anything to break us up. I didn't want to believe
35	it, but now I see it's true.

1	KATE:	*(Found out, now she attempts to justify her actions.)* **Well,**
2		**can you blame me? The guy's a jerk. He has more**
3		**overnight guests than Holiday Inn.**
4	CARA:	That's just rumor. I know the truth. I know David.
5	KATE:	So, what you're saying is you believe him and not me.
6	CARA:	I'm saying I don't understand you. You'd think, as my
7		best friend, you'd want me to be happy.
8	KATE:	Well, you'd think so, huh?
9	CARA:	Yes.
10	KATE:	Well, then, why don't you show me the same consid-
11		eration?
12	CARA:	Excuse me?
13	KATE:	*You!* All you care about is you. You have been like
14		this ever since I have known you. It's always, "Kate,
15		you're my best friend. Kate, what would I do without you.
16		Kate, can I come over? I need to talk to someone who
17		really understands me." But, when you have a boyfriend,
18		right away it's, "Kate, get lost. So-and-so and I are busy
19		tonight." When you have a man, you are like a horse with
20		blinders. It's all you see.
21	CARA:	That's not true.
22	KATE:	Oh, isn't it? Where were you when I needed you?
23		When my parents were first getting divorced and I had
24		no one to talk to?
25	CARA:	I was there for you all the time.
26	KATE:	The hell you were. That was when you were going out
27		with Andrew. Twenty-four hours a day, Andrew this,
28		Andrew that. Thank God you two broke up before the
29		divorce papers were signed so you could spend some time
30		with me. Of course, as I recall, we spent most of that time
31		talking about how unhappy you were because you two
32		had broken up. Oh, you were so "at one" with my mother
33		and her divorce. You were so "simpatico" as you liked to
34		say.
35	CARA:	Well, I could understand what she was going through.

1   My heart was breaking, too.

2 KATE: Cara, you and Andrew went out for three months.

3   Three lousy little months. My family was falling apart

4   and I had no one to talk to.

5 CARA: Well, I'm sorry, but the world does not revolve around

6   you.

7 KATE: You know, you're right. It doesn't revolve around any

8   of us, though. Something you have yet to learn. I suppose

9   what I did with David was pretty stupid, yes. But I

10   thought that maybe if he fell back to his old ways and

11   got together with me, you two would break up and I would

12   have my old friend back. But, guess what? I don't need

13   that kind of friendship. You want David? Fine. I wish you

14   all the best. I'm tired of being there for you while you

15   are never there for me. You take up too much emotional

16   energy. Maybe that's why you and all your boyfriends

17   last only a short while.

18 CARA: Well, at least I have boyfriends.

19 KATE: *(Quietly, caught off guard)* Very nice, Cara. You know

20   where to strike, don't you?

21 CARA: I didn't mean that. I'm just angry.

22 KATE: Well, maybe you're right. I don't have a boyfriend.

23   But maybe my standards are a little higher than yours.

24   I'm not willing to settle for anyone just to have someone

25   to call a boyfriend.

26 CARA: *(Getting angry all over again)* Willing to settle? Face it,

27   Kate, you just haven't got anyone interested in you. You'd

28   be thrilled to have someone, but you don't, so you take

29   your petty jealousies out on me.

30 KATE: Believe what you want.

31 CARA: Who was going after whose boyfriend?

32 KATE: OK, I'll admit that one. However, I thought I had a

33   reason to do so. I'll also admit it was the wrong thing to

34   do. It was a stupid reason, and I apologize . . .

35 CARA: Thank you. I accept your apology. Now maybe . . .

1   **KATE:**   *(Letting her anger come out, cutting her off)* **However,**
2   **that's all I apologize for, misguided concern for a friend.**
3   **But you know what? I was more misguided about who**
4   **my friend was. I just realized how truly shallow you are.**
5   **You wouldn't know how to be a true friend if your life**
6   **depended on it. I'm tired of watching you hang on some**
7   **guy, of listening to the many stories you tell about all the**
8   **things you go through. I'm sick of always being there for**
9   **you and your never being there for me. I'm just plain sick**
10   **of you.**
11   **CARA:**   **Well, I'm sick of you too. I'm tired of your moping**
12   **around when I'm with a guy. It's weird. You get strange**
13   **and quiet. I know you're jealous, but it's weird. Get your**
14   **own life, get your own boyfriend.**
15   **KATE:**   **I don't want a boyfriend.**
16   **CARA:**   **Maybe because you just can't get one.**
17   **KATE:**   **I just don't want one. I don't need one.**
18   **CARA:**   **Maybe that's your problem right there.**
19   **KATE:**   **What is?**
20   **CARA:**   **That you don't want a boyfriend.**
21   **KATE:**   **What I want is none of your business.**
22   **CARA:**   **Don't you think it a little strange that the only time**
23   **we ever fight is when I am going out with someone?**
24   **KATE:**   **And what, exactly, are you trying to say?**
25   **CARA:**   **I'm not trying to say anything. I am simply pointing**
26   **out what is becoming a pretty obvious fact.**
27   **KATE:**   **What *fact* is that, Cara?**
28   **CARA:**   **The fact that you have never had a boyfriend. The**
29   **fact that you get very possessive of my time when I do.**
30   **The fact that you are only really angry at me when I talk**
31   **about when I am with a guy. And you never talk about**
32   **guys. I find that rather strange, now that I think about it.**
33   **KATE:**   *(A deadly pause)* **I think that this conversation has**
34   **come to an end.**
35   **CARA:**   *(Looking at her evenly, unsure of what to say)* **I think so, too.**

1   **KATE:** *(Gathering her things)* **I don't think we really have**
2   **anything left to say to one another.**
3   **CARA:** **Neither do I.**
4   **KATE:** *(Beginning to leave, she stops, her back to CARA.)* **This is**
5   **your last chance to take back that comment. It's your**
6   **last chance to save whatever friendship we have.**
7   **CARA:** **Think about what I said, Kate. Maybe there's some**
8   **truth to it.**
9   **KATE:** *(Turning to face CARA, a pause and then)* **Good-bye, Cara.**
10   **CARA:** **Good-bye, Kate.** *(KATE exits, quietly.)* **Think about it,**
11   **Kate.**
12
13
14
15
16
17
18
19
20
21
22
23
24
25
26
27
28
29
30
31
32
33
34
35

GOD IS A MAN

1
2
3 **TAMARA:** A bit "under the weather."
4 **ANGELA:** Tamara's commiserating friend.
5 **KOURTNEY:** Practical, to the point.
6 **SETTING:** Study hall, after school.
7
8 TAMARA: *(Inching her way to the floor)* **Oooh, yuck. Dying. I'm**
9   **dying.**
10 ANGELA: *(Looking up from her book)* **What's wrong with you?**
11 TAMARA: **Cramps. Serious cramps.**
12 KOURTNEY: **Tamara, I told you not to take those aspirin,**
13   **didn't I? My doctor said aspirin only makes it worse.**
14 TAMARA: *(Moaning)* **Crrraaammppsss.**
15 KOURTNEY: **Sorry, no sympathy from me.**
16 ANGELA: **For goodness sake, Kourtney. You don't have to**
17   **be so heartless. Can't you see she's in pain?**
18 KOURTNEY: **Yeah. It's not like it's something she and every**
19   **other woman in the world hasn't experienced already.**
20   *(To TAMARA)* **Suck it up. Quit whining.**
21 TAMARA: *(Whining)* **I'm not whining. I'm in pain.**
22 KOURTNEY: **No, you're uncomfortable. I think real pain will**
23   **happen when you're in labor.**
24 TAMARA: **Not for many, many years, maybe never, if it's**
25   **anything like this.**
26 ANGELA: **My sister Meredith just had her baby. Twenty-two**
27   **hours of hard labor. Then they ended up doing a C-section.**
28 TAMARA: **Twenty-two hours?**
29 KOURTNEY: **My mom said that it was like having big-time**
30   **cramps for hours and hours at regular intervals.**
31 ANGELA: **Meredith said that while she was in labor, the only**
32   **thought that kept her sane was all of the horrible pain**
33   **she was going to inflict upon her husband when she was**
34   **through it, and all of the various ways she would inflict it.**
35 TAMARA: **I would love to have a man go through this at least**

1   once.
2   KOURTNEY: Hah! They couldn't take it. They whine if they
3   get a splinter. Can you imagine any of them going through
4   this once a month?
5   ANGELA: Please. My father takes to his bed if he has a
6   headache.
7   TAMARA: My brother! He's the same way. Last week he had a
8   cold. You would have thought that he was dying the way
9   he carried on. God! If I could just give him these cramps
10   once before I die, it would make it all worthwhile.
11   KOURTNEY: I'm telling you, God's a man.
12   ANGELA: What?
13   KOURTNEY: Think about it. Who gets cramps? Women. Who
14   has to carry a baby for nine months? Women. Who has
15   to go through labor? Women. Who always has to wait in
16   mile-long lines to use the bathroom? Women. If God were
17   a woman, she would have thought of a much better way
18   to go about all of this.
19   ANGELA: That is so true.
20   TAMARA: You're right, Kourtney. And who holds all of this
21   over our heads and makes us miserable?
22   ALL THREE: *Men!*
23   ANGELA: God, things would be so different if men had to go
24   through what women go through.
25   TAMARA: How?
26   KOURTNEY: OK, I've got an example. If men had periods, then
27   they would use it to point out that women have no sense
28   of time because they are not equipped with an inner clock.
29   ANGELA: Not only that, they probably would have figured
30   out a way to take it out, hang it someplace and come back
31   for it a week later when it was done, thus eliminating
32   cramps altogether.
33   TAMARA: Why haven't they come up with that now? When I
34   *need* it?
35   KOURTNEY: Because God's a . . .

1   **ALL THREE:** *Man!*

2   **ANGELA:** You know what else really bugs me? When you're

3   in a foul mood and some guy attributes it to PMS. Can

4   women never just be in a foul mood? Do they have to

5   turn it into this fully sexist thing?

6   **KOURTNEY:** No kidding. I, for one, have never experienced

7   PMS.

8   **TAMARA:** *(Looking at ANGELA with a raised eyebrow, who*

9   *returns the look)* **Uh-huh. Certainly.**

10   **KOURTNEY:** Shut up! I haven't.

11   **ANGELA:** Of course not.

12   **KOURTNEY:** I haven't. Never. Sometimes I just feel foul.

13   **TAMARA:** That's right, Angela. Sometimes she just feels foul.

14   About the fifteenth of every month.

15   **KOURTNEY:** Shut up! Just shut up! You guys are so rude. I

16   hate you sometimes! I would never talk about you like

17   that. *(She begins to get teary.)* I thought you were my friends,

18   my support group.

19   **ANGELA:** Somebody check a calendar.

20   **KOURTNEY:** *(Getting wild)* You don't have to check any

21   calendar. I don't have PMS. Can't a person get angry or

22   upset when she finds her best friends are betraying her?

23   **TAMARA:** It's the fifteenth.

24   **KOURTNEY:** *(Looking at them both, sitting back down and*

25   *laughing in embarrassment)* **Oh, man. Dammit.** *(Shaking her*

26   *fist to the heavens)* **You could have thought of a better way,**

27   I'm telling you!

28   **TAMARA:** Well, look on the bright side. At least we have an

29   excuse. Guys just have moods to have them.

30   **ANGELA:** You should have seen Kevin today in class. What

31   an idiot.

32   **KOURTNEY:** What'd he do?

33   **TAMARA:** Oh, it was ridiculous. He sat in the back, his black

34   mood hanging over him like a storm cloud.

35   **ANGELA:** I know! I saw him sitting there, all alone. So I went

1   up and asked him what was wrong. Of course, he gave
2   the standard answer . . .
3 ALL THREE: *(Mimicking a whining male)* **Nothing.**
4 TAMARA: Don't you hate that? If nothing is wrong, then
5   don't sit there and look miserable.
6 ANGELA: It was such a pitiful, pathetic cry for attention.
7 TAMARA: I was embarrassed for him.
8 KOURTNEY: Did he say what was wrong?
9 ANGELA: After I did the usual prodding one has to do to get
10   any male to communicate.
11 TAMARA: A nauseating display.
12 ANGELA: No kidding. Anyway, he got into a fight with
13   Rhonda.
14 KOURTNEY: Big deal. They always fight.
15 ANGELA: But this time he claims it's over for good.
16 KOURTNEY: For the thousandth time.
17 TAMARA: Well, I talked to Rhonda, and she said the same
18   thing.
19 ANGELA: She did? I didn't hear that!
20 KOURTNEY: Tell everything.
21 TAMARA: Well, she told me that she was tired of his mood
22   swings. He apparently had the nerve to tell her that if
23   she had any kind of feminine sensitivity that she would
24   be able to pick up on his "vibes."
25 ANGELA: "Vibes"? He actually said "vibes"?
26 TAMARA: Can you believe it? Anyway, he said that because
27   she is a woman and should be nurturing, she should be
28   able to intuitively pick up on his moods and understand
29   him without him having to spell it out for her.
30 KOURTNEY: Get me a gun. I'm gonna kill me a pig.
31 ANGELA: The nerve. The absolute nerve. What'd she do?
32 TAMARA: She told him that she was tired of his stupidity
33   and that the only intuition she had was the one that told
34   her to get out of this relationship before she killed him.
35 KOURTNEY: Good for her!

1   ANGELA: And this is the man that wants to be senior class
2   president?
3   KOURTNEY: Not in my lifetime, I am here to tell you. Hell,
4   I'll run before I'll vote for him!
5   ANGELA: Really! *(She pauses and considers.)* Really?
6   TAMARA: *(Catching on to ANGELA's idea)* Yeah? Yeah!
7   KOURTNEY: What? *(Seeing their meaning)* No, no way. Not
8   me. Unh-unh.
9   ANGELA: For someone who is always talking about women
10   taking control, maybe you should.
11   TAMARA: I think it's a great idea.
12   KOURTNEY: No way. Absolutely not.
13   ANGELA: Why?
14   KOURTNEY: Because ... because ... I   don't   know,   just
15   because.
16   TAMARA: Are you afraid?
17   KOURTNEY: Of what?
18   TAMARA: That what they say is true? That a woman couldn't
19   do the job?
20   KOURTNEY: You   will   stop   right   now.   That's   a   stupid
21   argument.
22   ANGELA: Is it? Maybe Kevin is right.
23   KOURTNEY: About what?
24   ANGELA: That women are just too soft for the job. That they
25   don't have the inner strength.
26   KOURTNEY: He said that?
27   TAMARA: Right after the comment about real women should
28   be able to aid their men to achieve their life's goal.
29   ANGELA: Maybe that's the real reason he and Rhonda broke
30   up. She just doesn't know how to be supportive of her
31   man.
32   KOURTNEY: Excuse me?! "Aid her man"? What about the
33   woman's goal? And what about supporting the woman to
34   achieve hers?
35   ANGELA: Apparently, you don't have any, do you?

1   KOURTNEY: I could achieve a goal I set up for myself.

2   TAMARA: And what goal might that be?

3   KOURTNEY: I see where this is going. You're just trying to

4   goad me into running against Kevin for class president.

5   ANGELA: *(Getting excited)* That's right! And think how great

6   that would be. There hasn't been a woman class officer

7   at this school in years.

8   TAMARA: Not since we've been going here.

9   ANGELA: Not since my sister Meredith graduated, which

10   was almost ten years ago.

11   TAMARA: *(Talking fast)* Think about it, Kourtney, you could

12   be a woman with a new vision . . .

13   ANGELA: One to take us into the twenty-first century and

14   beyond . . .

15   TAMARA: You could set standards that most men would

16   envy . . .

17   ANGELA: We could get a whole slate going!

18   TAMARA: I bet Rhonda would run for treasurer!

19   KOURTNEY: *(Catching their excitement)* Jessica would be great

20   as secretary. And Julia would be a terrific vice president.

21   TAMARA: Angela and I could run your campaign!

22   ANGELA: We could organize all the women on campus.

23   Mobilize for unity!

24   KOURTNEY: *(Thinking)* We could really do this, couldn't we?

25   *(She looks at their eager faces.)* We could! But I can't do it

26   alone. I need your help.

27   TAMARA: Do you even have to ask?

28   ANGELA: *(Mimicking Kevin)* Hey, Kourt, I'm picking up on

29   your vibes. *(All three laugh.)*

30   KOURTNEY: I know Rhonda would do it, just to make a

31   point to Kevin, but do you think Jess and Julia would go

32   for it?

33   TAMARA: Oh, yeah. They're really into making a difference

34   at the school.

35   ANGELA: And would this make a difference? A full slate of

1   women running the senior class.
2   **KOURTNEY:** *(Taking a deep breath)* **OK. Let's do it.**
3   **TAMARA: You're serious.**
4   **KOURTNEY: Very.**
5   **ANGELA: I'll call the others. We'll get started tonight.**
6   **TAMARA: This could really happen, huh?**
7   **KOURTNEY: Could? It will. We'll make it happen.**
8   **ANGELA:** *(Very matter of fact, no embellishment)* **We are woman,**
9   **hear us roar.**
10 **KOURTNEY: We are people, see us win!**
11
12
13
14
15
16
17
18
19
20
21
22
23
24
25
26
27
28
29
30
31
32
33
34
35

THE TOAST

SUZANNE, NATALIE, ALYSHA: All age 18.

SETTING: Kitchen. Three girls, friends, confidants, spending the last weekend before high school graduation together. SUZANNE, NATALIE (accent on the second syllable) and ALYSHA.

SUZANNE: **OK, OK, who am I?** *(She takes a large swig out of her bottle, burps loudly and falls on her face. ALYSHA and NATALIE fall over laughing.)*

NATALIE: **I know, I know . . . it's David.**

ALYSHA: **No! No! It's Ray.**

SUZANNE: **Nope! It's *me* at Julie's party last weekend.** *(The girls again explode in slightly drunken laughter.)*

ALYSHA: **You are such a little piggy, Suzanne.**

SUZANNE: **Yeah, well, gimme those chips.** *(She takes the chip bowl and buries her face in it, gobbling.)* **Snort, snort.**

NATALIE: **Look at us. Just the picture of three grown-up women about to graduate.**

SUZANNE: *(Holding her bottle high in a toast)* **To the grown-up girls.**

NATALIE: **To us!**

ALYSHA: **And the women we will become.** *(They drink.)*

SUZANNE: **You know, I shouldn't be eating all this garbage food, but the way I see it, pretty soon all my decisions will be grown-up ones. We graduate next week and I want to spend one last night with my very, very best friends getting very, very drunk and eating as much chocolate as is humanly possible. Pass me those M & Ms.**

NATALIE: **Drink up, ladies, because we may never pass this way again.**

ALYSHA: **Can you believe how fast the last four years have gone? God, remember being a freshman?**

1   **SUZANNE:**   Nope. **Right now, I can barely remember my**
2   **name.**
3   **NATALIE:**   *(Looking at them, getting a bit weepy)* **You two are my**
4   **very best friends in the whole world. I want you to know**
5   **that I love you both like sisters.**
6   **SUZANNE:**   *(Getting misty eyed)* **You are so sweet.** *(She hugs both*
7   *of them in a headlock.)* **You are both so sweet.**
8   **ALYSHA:**   So are you, Suzanne. **And you, too, Nat.** *(She, too,*
9   *begins to get misty.)* **I will never forget this night as long**
10   **as I live.**
11   **NATALIE:**   Me, either.
12   **SUZANNE:**   I know I will always remember it . . . or at least I
13   **will try.** *(She laughs almost wildly and drinks again.)*
14   **NATALIE:**   **I think our young friend has had more than her**
15   **share of wine coolers tonight.** *(She reaches for SUZANNE's*
16   *bottle.)*
17   **SUZANNE:**   *(Shooting away with it)* **I don't think so. I will decide**
18   **when I have had enough.** *(She stands, sways, sits back down.)*
19   **I have now decided that I have had enough.**
20   **ALYSHA:**   **I have never seen you drink so much before,**
21   **Suzanne.**
22   **SUZANNE:**   Yeah, well . . .
23   **NATALIE:**   Oh, Alysha, leave her alone. **Quit being such a**
24   **mother hen.**
25   **ALYSHA:**   I'm not. I just said . . .
26   **SUZANNE:**   That I was drinking too much. **So what? So the**
27   **hell what? What business is it of yours anyway?**
28   **ALYSHA:**   It's not. I just was making a comment.
29   **SUZANNE:**   *(Taking another drink)* **Well, comment on someone**
30   **else from now on.**
31   **NATALIE:**   What wild hair crawled up you, Suzanne?
32   **SUZANNE:**   Excuse me?
33   **NATALIE:**   Well, for God's sake, she just barely mentioned how
34   **much you were drinking.**
35   **SUZANNE:**   You know, I don't need to listen to this. **I can go**

1   **home and hear this kind of talk.** *(She grabs her purse and*
2   *starts off, pulling out her car keys.)*
3   **ALYSHA:**   **Oh, no you don't. You are in no condition to drive.**
4   **Hell, none of us are.** *(She begins to giggle.)*
5   **SUZANNE:**   *(Pushing ALYSHA, in a rage)* **Don't tell me what**
6   **to do!**
7   **NATALIE:**   *(Grabbing SUZANNE and her keys)* **Like hell we**
8   **won't. I've had far less to drink than you, and I know I**
9   **can't drive, so don't tell me you can.**
10   **ALYSHA:**   *(Grabbing at the wobbly, angry SUZANNE)* **You are not**
11   **taking the car, so forget about it.** *(There is a moment of*
12   *tension, as NATALIE watches them struggle for the keys*
13   *then . . .)*
14   **NATALIE:**   *(Yelling)* **Don't take the car, you'll kill youself!** *(All*
15   *three look at each other for a moment and then erupt in laughter,*
16   *the tension eased. SUZANNE sits between them.)*
17   **SUZANNE:**   **You know, I'm not as drunk as I'm acting. I'm**
18   **really not. I just want to be drunk tonight. I want to be**
19   **as drunk as a human being can get without throwing up.**
20   **But I don't want to not remember tonight. This is our**
21   **last night, forever and ever just being with each other**
22   **like this, you know?**
23   **ALYSHA:**   **I know. You two are so special to me. After four**
24   **years of high school, boyfriends, teachers, stupid classes,**
25   **divorced parents, and everything else, I can't believe**
26   **we're finally out of here.**
27   **NATALIE:**   **Off to college, career, maybe husbands and**
28   **families.**
29   **SUZANNE:**   **Maybe? Nah, for sure.**
30   **ALYSHA:**   **Hey, my Mr. Right is coming, I know for sure. So's**
31   **yours and Suzanne's. We just have to wait and be picky.**
32   **NATALIE:**   **No lowering standards for us. Right?** *(She holds up*
33   *her bottle in a toast.)*
34   **ALYSHA:**   *(Holding her bottle up to join in the toast)* **Right!**
35   **SUZANNE:**   **God, I hope so.** *(She toasts, too, and then breaks into*

1   *tears.)* **Oh, God, oh, God, oh, God. I didn't want to do this.**
2   **ALYSHA:** **What's wrong?**
3   **NATALIE:** **Suzanne, what's the matter?**
4   **ALYSHA:** *(Taking the crying SUZANNE in her arms)* **Suzanne,**
5   **what is it?**
6   **SUZANNE:** **I didn't want to tell you tonight, because tonight**
7   **was supposed to be just for us. Just the three of us having**
8   **our own private party that we would always remember**
9   **as special. But . . .**
10   **ALYSHA:** **Suzanne, what is it?**
11   **SUZANNE:** *(Wiping her eyes)* **It's good news. Really, it is.**
12   **NATALIE:** **OK, then tell us.**
13   **SUZANNE:** *(Taking a deep breath)* **David asked me to marry**
14   **him . . .**
15   **NATALIE:** **No way!**
16   **ALYSHA:** **Your first marriage proposal.** *Omigod!* **This is so**
17   **exciting.**
18   **NATALIE:** **I can't believe it.**
19   **ALYSHA:** **You didn't answer him yet, did you?**
20   **NATALIE:** **Of course she didn't. This is something you savor**
21   **and share with your very best friends before you turn**
22   **him down. Why weren't you going to tell us tonight?**
23   **Tonight is the perfect night to tell us.**
24   **SUZANNE:** **Because, I did answer him, and I knew you guys**
25   **would get mad that I hadn't told you yet.**
26   **ALYSHA:** **Some friend you are. So, what did you say? How did**
27   **you turn him down?**
28   **NATALIE:** **Were you sweet, or cold, or confused . . . what?**
29   **ALYSHA:** **We want every single detail.**
30   **SUZANNE:** *(Quietly)* **I told him yes.**
31   **ALYSHA:** *(After a moment's look at SUZANNE)* **You did what?**
32   **SUZANNE:** **I told him yes.**
33   **NATALIE:** **You did not. You wouldn't.**
34   **SUZANNE:** **But I did.**
35   **ALYSHA:** **How can you get married?**

1	SUZANNE: I'm eighteen years old, Alysha. I can make my
2	own decisions.
3	NATALIE: Do you love him?
4	SUZANNE: I'm marrying him, what do you think?
5	NATALIE: Do you love him?
6	SUZANNE: He's good-looking, rich, really, really nice. Why
7	shouldn't I love him?
8	ALYSHA: But do you?
9	SUZANNE: *(Getting angry)* Why do you keep asking me that?
10	*(Becoming more emphatic with each sentence)* Yes, I love him.
11	I love him with all my heart and soul and every fiber of
12	my being. *I love David* ... *(She bursts into tears)* and I'm
13	pregnant.
14	ALYSHA: *(A quiet moment of shock, then)* Oh, no.
15	NATALIE: Are you sure?
16	SUZANNE: Yes. I took a home pregnancy test. It was positive.
17	NATALIE: Sometimes they're wrong.
18	SUZANNE: Not five times. I'm pregnant.
19	ALYSHA: This is why you're marrying David?
20	SUZANNE: What else can I do?
21	NATALIE: There are other things.
22	SUZANNE: Abortion? *(The girls nod.)* I thought about it. I
23	really did. But I can't. I just can't. It's OK for other people,
24	but I just can't. I wish I could.
25	NATALIE: Have you told your parents?
26	SUZANNE: Yeah.
27	ALYSHA: What'd they say?
28	SUZANNE: David was with me. I thought my father was
29	going to kill him, but when we told them we were getting
30	married, everyone seemed to calm down. Mom cried. I
31	cried.
32	ALYSHA: You don't have to marry him, you know.
33	SUZANNE: What do you suggest I do? Single mother? I don't
34	think so.
35	NATALIE: There's adoption.

1	SUZANNE:	I couldn't. No way. Knowing that I had a child out
2		there somewhere and never knowing who she was or
3		what she was doing? No.
4	ALYSHA:	The bottom line, though, is do you love David?
5	SUZANNE:	You mean does my heart go pitter pat when he
6		walks into a room? No. But can I count on him? Is he
7		good to me? Will he take care of things? Yes.
8	NATALIE:	That's not love.
9	SUZANNE:	Maybe it is, in its own way.
10	ALYSHA:	That ain't love in my book, girlfriend.
11	SUZANNE:	Maybe it's not teenage passion, and being all hot
12		and bothered, but it is all I have right now. Maybe it's
13		all I can expect.
14	NATALIE:	Is it enough?
15	SUZANNE:	I will make it be enough.
16	ALYSHA:	I don't understand how you can do this. Does David
17		know how you feel?
18	SUZANNE:	Yes, but he wants to do the right thing.
19	ALYSHA:	The right thing is to not be pregnant.
20	SUZANNE:	A little late.
21	ALYSHA:	You know, I can't believe this. This is the most
22		selfish thing you have ever done.
23	SUZANNE:	What?
24	ALYSHA:	I told you not to sleep with him. I told you! But you
25		wouldn't listen.
26	NATALIE:	Alysha, back off.
27	ALYSHA:	No, Natalie, I won't back off. Both of us told her
28		that, but, as usual, she didn't listen to us. Now look at
29		her. She's going to have a baby, she's getting married.
30		Her life is over.
31	NATALIE:	Or just beginning.
32	ALYSHA:	What?
33	NATALIE:	Maybe, just maybe, what Suzanne is doing is the
34		right thing for her. Maybe she and David will make this
35		work and will live a long and terrific life together. Maybe

1   they will be happy and have more children and make a
2   lovely successful life for themselves.
3   ALYSHA: And maybe I'll grow wings and fly to Jupiter
4   tonight, too.
5   SUZANNE: I know the obstacles I'm facing. I'm not stupid . . .
6   ALYSHA: Just careless.
7   SUZANNE: OK. But my decision is made.
8   ALYSHA: But is it the right one?
9   SUZANNE: I don't know. I know I'm scared. And angry that
10   I have to make this kind of decision . . .
11   ALYSHA: This does not make for a great marital foundation.
12   SUZANNE: I'm aware of that, Alysha.
13   NATALIE: Suzanne, can you really spend the rest of your
14   life with someone you don't love?
15   SUZANNE: I didn't say I didn't love him. I don't know how I
16   feel. I guess I will find out, huh?
17   ALYSHA: I think you're making a big mistake.
18   SUZANNE: What do you think, Natalie?
19   NATALIE: I don't know. I hope you know what you're doing.
20   SUZANNE: I think I'm making an adult choice now.
21   ALYSHA: It's your life and your choice.
22   NATALIE: *(Holding her bottle)* To us.
23   SUZANNE: The grown-up girls.
24   ALYSHA: And the women we might have become. *(They tap*
25   *their bottles, and hold them, without drinking, each lost in her*
26   *own thoughts.)*
27
28
29
30
31
32
33
34
35

THE KITTEN HAS CLAWS

AMANDA: A senior, supportive of her friend.

SHARON: A senior, possessive about her male friends.

AMY: A pretty sophomore, very self-confident.

SETTING: The scene opens as SHARON and AMANDA stand talking quietly to each other. AMY enters the room and both SHARON and AMANDA bristle angrily. The playing area could be a bathroom or perhaps a backstage area.

AMANDA: Sharon, look over there. It's Amy.

SHARON: Where? *(She spots her, and shakes her head in disgust.)*

AMANDA: Look at the little tramp. Who does she think she is, anyway?

SHARON: The guys' favorite, that's who.

AMANDA: Favorite what is what I want to know.

SHARON: I think we know what she's the favorite for. *(They laugh nastily and continue to watch as she primps before a make-up mirror and watches the two out of the corner of her eye.)*

AMANDA: Come on, let's go. There's nothing to see here.

SHARON: Yeah. *(She starts off with AMANDA.)* Wait.

AMANDA: What?

SHARON: Why should I leave?

AMANDA: Because we're late to class.

SHARON: But it looks like she comes in and so I leave. No. No way. I'm staying.

AMANDA: Sharon, we're late for class.

SHARON: I don't care. It's the principle of the situation. We don't leave until she does.

AMANDA: Whatever. *(She sits and they both stare at AMY. This goes on for a while as AMY becomes ever more uncomfortable with them staring at her. Finally:)*

AMY: What? What are you looking at?

SHARON: Not much.

AMY: Well, just stop it.

1   SHARON: So, now the little sophomore is telling the seniors
2   what to do? I don't think so.
3   AMANDA: Learn your place, little girl.
4   AMY: Amanda, I have never done anything to either of you,
5   so why don't you two just leave me alone?
6   SHARON: Oh, you've never done anything, huh? How about
7   trying to steal our boyfriends?
8   AMY: I never steal anyone's boyfriend.
9   SHARON: Oh, please. You throw yourself at every guy in this
10   school.
11   AMY: I smile at them. I can't help it if they find me attractive.
12   AMANDA: Attractive. Is that what they are calling it these
13   days?
14   SHARON: We've always called it by a different word. Now,
15   Amanda, what is that word? Could it be ... *slut*?
16   AMANDA: I think so, Sharon. Yes, *slut* is the word.
17   AMY: Why don't you two just leave me alone?
18   SHARON: *(Closing in on her)* Why don't you just leave?
19   AMY: I have just as much right to be here as anyone.
20   SHARON: Not while I'm here you don't.
21   AMY: Who says?
22   SHARON: Me.
23   AMY: And who are you? Who says you are the queen around
24   here?
25   SHARON: When it comes to power at this school, little girl,
26   I have quite a bit more than you. I can make you or break
27   you.
28   AMANDA: It's true, Amy, so watch your step.
29   SHARON: And when I say leave, I suggest you do just that
30   ... little girl.
31   AMY: Make me.
32   SHARON: *(Moving toward her)* I'd be happy to.
33   AMY: *(Not backing away)* Go ahead.
34   SHARON: *(Surprised by this)* I said leave.
35   AMY: And I said make me.

1	AMANDA: You better go, Amy.
2	AMY: Why? What's she going to do? Beat me up? I doubt it.
3	AMANDA: She just might.
4	AMY: No, she won't, will you, Sharon? Not as a senior so
5	close to graduation. Not with recommendations still to
6	be written and college applications to be sent. She's got
7	too much to lose. While I, on the other hand, as a
8	sophomore, have nothing to lose. Oh, maybe a three- or
9	four-day suspension, but that's not much. So, go ahead,
10	Sharon, make me.
11	AMANDA: Oh, the kitten has claws.
12	AMY: And she's not afraid to use them.
13	SHARON: You're right. I won't fight. But I can make your life
14	around here pretty miserable.
15	AMY: Oh? How?
16	SHARON: Watch me. *(She walks away.)*
17	AMY: Watch *me.*
18	SHARON: *(With her back to AMY)* Excuse me?
19	AMY: I said watch me.
20	AMANDA: And the kitten's claws are sharp.
21	SHARON: *(To AMY)* What does that mean?
22	AMY: Guess who walked me to class today? Sean.
23	SHARON: No way.
24	AMANDA: That's who that was ...
25	SHARON: What?
26	AMANDA: I saw him. I just didn't know it was him. I guess he
27	saw me and ran around the corner.
28	AMY: It was Sean.
29	SHARON: Why did he run?
30	AMY: Because he obviously didn't want you to know he was
31	walking me to class. *(Nastily sweet)* I think it's only fair
32	that you should know.
33	SHARON: *(To AMANDA)* Are you sure?
34	AMANDA: It was him. I know it was.
35	SHARON: Then why didn't you say anything?

1 AMANDA: I wasn't sure till she said something, then it
2   clicked in my mind that it was him.
3 SHARON: *(To AMY)* You stay away from him, do you hear
4   me?
5 AMY: *(Derisively)* Please, I don't even like him. I can't help it
6   if he wanted to walk me to class, however.
7 SHARON: Make sure in the future that you do, little girl.
8 AMY: You see, *big girl,* there is the difference between us.
9   I don't *tell* people what to do. I simply behave like a lady,
10   something you obviously don't. And you will notice that
11   Sean is walking me to class, like I didn't tell him, and I'm
12   still here, unlike you told me to do.
13 SHARON: Listen to me . . .
14 AMY: No, you listen to me. You walk around this school like
15   you think everyone admires and respects you. Well, they
16   don't. Most of us laugh at you. So, Sharon, back off, or
17   you will find yourself in a lot of trouble.
18 SHARON: Is that a threat?
19 AMY: No, it's a promise.
20 AMANDA: You know, you do have to go off campus sometime.
21 AMY: Anytime you see me, feel free to come right up. You two
22   don't scare me at all. In fact, if anything, you amuse me.
23 SHARON: Amuse?
24 AMY: At the least, amuse. At the most, you two are laughable.
25   *(She turns to leave and walks out of the room. SHARON and*
26   *AMANDA watch silently.)*
27 AMANDA: What just happened here?
28 SHARON: I don't know.
29 AMANDA: Was there a fight?
30 SHARON: Yeah, and I think we lost.
31 AMANDA: This is weird.
32 SHARON: I feel suddenly too old for high school.
33 AMANDA: Me too.
34 SHARON: Let's go to class.
35 AMANDA: Yeah. One more tardy in government and I'm

1   going to lose a unit.

2   **SHARON:**   **I have to ask Mr. Liggett for a letter of recommen-**

3   **dation for UCLA.** *(They begin to walk out; both stop and look*

4   *at the spot where they were.)* **This was so weird.**

5

6

7

8

9

10

11

12

13

14

15

16

17

18

19

20

21

22

23

24

25

26

27

28

29

30

31

32

33

34

35

POINT OF VIEW

ANDREA: Age 17, insecure and oversensitive.

LYNN: Age 17, also insecure and easily offended.

YVETTE: Age 17, secure, honest, diplomatic.

SETTING: ANDREA, YVETTE, and LYNN are together during the entire scene. However, there will be moments when two of the girls talk while one of the girls is in a freeze.

ANDREA: My hair. I hate my hair. If I curl it just a little bit, it flies all over. If I leave it, I look like I stuck my finger in a light socket.

YVETTE: You look fine. Quit worrying about it.

ANDREA: Don't tell me not to worry. Your hair does whatever you want it to. *I hate my hair!*

LYNN: My hair is never really a problem . . . *(Freeze)*

ANDREA: Did you hear Lynn today?

YVETTE: What about?

ANDREA: *(In a mocking voice)* My hair is never really a problem. Where does she get off? Who asked her?

YVETTE: What are you talking about?

ANDREA: Lynn. God, Yvette, don't you listen? She may as well have told me to shave myself bald.

YVETTE: I didn't hear that. She just said her hair doesn't give her any problems.

ANDREA: I know what I heard . . . *(LYNN unfreezes and the scene takes place again, but from ANDREA's view.)*

ANDREA: I hate my hair.

LYNN: I don't blame you.

ANDREA: What do you mean?

LYNN: If I were you, I would just cut that mop off and start fresh with a wig. It's hopeless. *(Laughs wildly, then freezes.)*

YVETTE: She said that?

ANDREA: Maybe not in those exact words, but that's what it felt like.

1   YVETTE: Maybe you should talk to her.
2   ANDREA: Maybe I will. *(LYNN unfreezes.)*
3   LYNN: So, did you guys see that dress Collanne was wearing
4   today?
5   ANDREA: It looked like something she stole out of the back
6   of a grocery store after the potatoes were stacked.
7   LYNN: *Omigod!* I know! How can she possibly think she
8   looks good in that?
9   ANDREA: Lynn, would you ever wear anything like that?
10   Yeah, maybe if tacky was your middle name . . . *(ANDREA*
11   *freezes.)*
12   LYNN: Yvette, I don't know about you, but I am getting very
13   tired of Andrea and her sneaky little remarks about my
14   clothes.
15   YVETTE: Huh?
16   LYNN: Listen, I know I'm not the best dressed person at
17   school, but I do what I can with what I have.
18   YVETTE: Andrea didn't say anything.
19   LYNN: God, Yvette, don't you listen? She practically called
20   my way of dressing tacky. *(ANDREA unfreezes and the scene*
21   *takes place from LYNN's point of view.)* Did you see that dress
22   Collanne had on today?
23   ANDREA: The potato sack number? That is the tackiest
24   thing I have ever seen in my life. It looks almost like that
25   dress you wore on Monday, Lynn.
26   LYNN: I don't have any dresses that look like that.
27   ANDREA: Oh, you're right. Yours don't say Idaho, they say
28   Gold Medal. *(Laughs wildly, then she freezes.)*
29   YVETTE: I think you're exaggerating, Lynn.
30   LYNN: Try paying attention once in a while.
31   YVETTE: Well, maybe you should talk to her.
32   LYNN: Maybe I will. *(ANDREA unfreezes.)*
33   ANDREA: So, anyway, where were you yesterday?
34   YVETTE: I was with Steve . . . *(She freezes.)*
35   LYNN: Oh, God, here we go again.

1   ANDREA: I am sick to death of hearing about the sainted
2   Steve.
3   LYNN: Tell me about it.
4   YVETTE: *(Unfreezing)* ... and we just stayed at my house
5   watching videos.
6   LYNN: Johnny came over to my house, too. He is Mr. Attitude
7   lately. All we do is fight anymore. He's always telling me
8   what to do and what to say. He acts like he's my father
9   more than my boyfriend.
10 ANDREA: You think you have it bad? Yesterday, Tony and I
11   were arguing and he grabbed me. Step back, huh? I told
12   him flat out, if he ever touched me like that again he
13   would be kissing pavement so fast and so hard he
14   wouldn't have any teeth left.
15 YVETTE: I don't know why you two put up with that kind of
16   treatment. *(She freezes.)*
17 ANDREA: Could you even believe Yvette today? Little Miss
18   High and Mighty.
19 LYNN: She thinks she is so perfect. Her and Saint Steven of
20   Fullerton.
21 ANDREA: Let us all pray.
22 LYNN: Did you hear her?
23 ANDREA: Miss Thing. *(YVETTE unfreezes and plays the scene*
24   *as the two girls remember it.)*
25 YVETTE: Steve came over yesterday. He's so perfect.
26 ANDREA: I was with Tony. He was in a little bit of a bad mood.
27 LYNN: Johnny was a little testy yesterday, too.
28 YVETTE: You two are crazy. If my Steve even thought about
29   crossing me, he would be out the door. He wouldn't dare
30   pull any kind of mood on me. You both are two of the
31   biggest wimps when it comes to your men. You need to
32   let them know who is boss, or they will walk all over you,
33   which apparently has already begun to occur. *(She*
34   *freezes.)*
35 ANDREA: One of these days, I am going to just slap her.

1   **LYNN:**   Let me know, and I'll hold her for you.

2   **YVETTE:**   *(Unfreezing)* **So, where are we going tonight?**

3   **ANDREA:**   There's that new club in town. Hot music and

4   majorly cute guys.

5   **LYNN:**   What about Tony?

6   **ANDREA:**   Just because we are going out doesn't mean I am

7   dead. I can still look, you know. *(Freezes.)*

8   **LYNN:**   *(To YVETTE, who smiles wanly)* **The tramp.** *(ANDREA*

9   *unfreezes.)* **Cute guys? I'm there!** *(Freezes.)*

10   **ANDREA:**   *(To YVETTE, who smiles wanly)* **The tramp.** *(LYNN*

11   *unfreezes.)* **About eight o'clock.**

12   **YVETTE:**   OK, but who's driving?

13   **ANDREA:**   I always drive. Someone else do it.

14   **LYNN:**   You don't always drive. I drive all the time.

15   **ANDREA:**   You do not. You hardly ever get the car. And I'm

16   always stuck hauling you all over town.

17   **LYNN:**   Oh, well, I'm sorry if it is such a chore. Maybe I just

18   won't go.

19   **YVETTE:**   Andrea didn't say that, Lynn.

20   **LYNN:**   Well, she may as well have. She's always commenting

21   on what I say and do.

22   **ANDREA:**   *Puhleese.* If anything, it's the other way around.

23   **LYNN:**   Oh, stop. You're the one.

24   **ANDREA:**   *(Overlapping)* Me? You are always saying things.

25   **LYNN:**   *(Overlapping)* I never talk about you.

26   **ANDREA and LYNN:**   Yvette, tell her.

27   **YVETTE:**   *(Wide-eyed innocence, desperately not wanting to make*

28   *trouble)* I ... uh ... *(She smiles, caught like a rabbit in a*

29   *headlight.)* Gee ... uh ... I ... well ...

30   **ANDREA:**   Come on, Yvette. Tell her you are just as sick of

31   her ways as I am.

32   **LYNN:**   My ways. You're the one. Yvette and I are both sick of

33   you.

34   **YVETTE:**   Uh ... I ... well ...

35   **LYNN and ANDREA:**   Say something, Yvette.

1 YVETTE: I think I should just keep my mouth shut and you
2   two should talk. *(She leaves.)*
3 LYNN: Can you believe her?
4 ANDREA: She practically told us to shut up.
5 LYNN: I know.
6 ANDREA: What's her problem lately?
7 LYNN: I didn't want to tell you this, but she is always talking
8   about you when you're not here.
9 ANDREA: Oh, my God. She does the same thing when you're
10   not around.
11 LYNN: The little traitor.
12 ANDREA: She just doesn't know the true meaning of friend-
13   ship, does she?
14 LYNN: Maybe we should talk to her.
15 ANDREA: Would she listen?
16 LYNN: Probably not.
17 ANDREA: It's just so typical.
18 LYNN: She's just jealous that we are such good friends.
19 ANDREA: I agree. She needs to grow up and be more like us.
20 LYNN: Honesty is the base for all real friendships.
21 ANDREA: She'll learn ... with time.
22
23
24
25
26
27
28
29
30
31
32
33
34
35

1   **BURNED**
2
3   *AMANDA, AMY, HEATHER:*   All lovely girls, close friends,
4   preparing for the annual Girl Date Dance.
5   *SETTING:*   AMANDA is fixing what looks very much like two
6   pirate costumes in her living room. She hums happily to herself
7   for a moment when she hears a knock at the door and goes to
8   answer it.
9
10   AMANDA: Just a minute.
11   HEATHER: *(Entering with AMY, both talking at the same time)* **I**
12   **can't believe you finally did it!**
13   AMY: **It's about time. So, what happened? How did you ask**
14   **him?**
15   HEATHER: **This is going to be so much fun. We can triple**
16   **date.**
17   AMY: **My dad already said we can use the van!**
18   AMANDA: **Better than that, my parents said I can stay out all**
19   **night after the dance. I don't have to be home until dawn.**
20   HEATHER: **This is going to be so much fun! OK, OK, OK,**
21   **tell me how you asked him!**
22   AMY: **I can't believe you finally got the nerve.**
23   AMANDA: **It wasn't easy, I can tell you that!**
24   HEATHER: **Thank God for Girl Date!**
25   AMANDA: **Really, if I had waited for Steve to ask me to a**
26   **dance, I'd never end up going.**
27   AMY: **I just think this is going to be so great. Me with Kevin,**
28   **Heather with David and now you with Steve. This is so**
29   **cool.**
30   HEATHER: **Especially because these guys are all like best**
31   **friends and so are we and we can all dress alike and go**
32   **out after and maybe go bowling in our outfits . . .**
33   AMANDA: **I'm making us the cutest outfits. Wait till you see . . .**
34   HEATHER: **. . . and then go to the beach and sit by a fire until**
35   **the police come and tell us about curfew and then we can**

54

1　　go to Denny's and have breakfast and play cards in the
2　　booth and end up staying up all night long . . .
3　AMY:　Take a breath, Heather.
4　HEATHER:　No, really. This is going to be so much fun.
5　AMANDA:　Steve told me that he is really looking forward to
6　　this dance, especially because it's the first time he and
7　　David and Kevin have ever tripled. He seemed really
8　　pleased that I asked him.
9　AMY:　*Sooo tell!*
10　AMANDA:　There's not much to tell.
11　HEATHER:　Listen, girl, I have spent countless hours
12　　building up your self-esteem and courage to get you to
13　　ask Steve to this stinkin' dance. If you think you are going
14　　to get by without telling me exactly what came down,
15　　you are sadly mistaken!
16　AMY:　I have to agree with Heather on this one, Amanda. So, talk.
17　AMANDA:　*(As they settle in)* OK. There's not that much to tell. I
18　　just asked him and he said yes.
19　AMY:　But what did you say?
20　HEATHER:　Exactly! Every word!
21　AMANDA:　Well . . . I just went up to him and started talking.
22　HEATHER:　What did you wear?
23　AMANDA:　That green sweater.
24　AMY:　Perfect! It totally brings out your eyes.
25　AMANDA:　I know, that's why I wore it. I figured he'd see that
26　　and how could he possibly turn me down? *(She laughs.)*
27　　No, really. I just remembered you saying how it makes
28　　my eyes look great! Anyway, I saw him standing with
29　　David and Kevin. They smiled, so I took courage from
30　　that and went on over.
31　HEATHER:　My David. He's so sweet.
32　AMY:　So's my Kevvy. He really likes you a lot, you know. I
33　　told him you were going to ask Steve and he said he
34　　thought for sure Steve would say yes.
35　AMANDA:　You *told* him?

1   AMY: Of course. I had to check out whether or not he'd say
2   yes, didn't I? I didn't want you to end up looking foolish.
3   AMANDA: Oh. Hmmm. I guess that's all right. Hmmm.
4   HEATHER: OK, OK, so then what? You see Steve with Kevin
5   and David. Did you ask him right in front of them?
6   AMANDA: No! I went up to the three of them and made small
7   talk for about twenty seconds . . .
8   HEATHER: Which is about all any man can handle . . .
9   AMANDA: Then I asked Steve to walk with me to class.
10   AMY: And then you asked him?
11   AMANDA: Well, almost. We walked to class and just kind of
12   didn't say anything for a while. It was kind of weird. It's
13   so easy to talk to him when we're all together in a group.
14   But one on one is strange.
15   HEATHER: Why?
16   AMANDA: I don't know. It was probably me, though, 'cause I
17   knew I wanted to ask him, and he probably knew I was
18   going to. So, we stood in front of Ms. San Paolo's room
19   for what seemed like forever and then I just kind of
20   brought it up.
21   HEATHER: How? What exactly did you say?
22   AMANDA: I don't remember exactly. Just something like,
23   "Steve, how'd you like to go to Girl Date with me?" and
24   then he said yes. That simple.
25   AMY: I knew he'd say yes!
26   AMANDA: He told me he doesn't have much money right
27   now, so I said I would get the outfits for it. Look. *(She*
28   *holds up what looks like two pirate costumes.)* **Aren't these**
29   **cute?**
30   HEATHER: Did you *make* these?
31   AMANDA: Uh-huh. It cost a little, but I figure what the heck,
32   it's worth it.
33   AMY: Don't you just love this desert island theme for this
34   dance?
35   AMANDA: And, look, I got you guys matching hats, too. This

1   way when we take our group picture we can all look alike!

2   **HEATHER:** *(Putting on a pirate hat)* **Omigod! You actually**

3   **made these? I can't believe how talented you are.**

4   **AMY:** *(Prancing around in hers, thrusting an imaginary sword)* **Ho,**

5   **me hearties, beware of Amy the scourge of the seven seas.**

6   **Arrr.**

7   **AMANDA: I thought we should go to the Jolly Roger for**

8   **dinner, too. In keeping with the whole idea.**

9   **HEATHER: This is too funny. The six of us going to dinner**

10   **at the Jolly Roger dressed as pirates. I *love* this whole**

11   **thing!**

12   **AMANDA:** *(The phone rings.)* **Oh, that's probably my aunt. I've**

13   **been working weekends for her just in case I got the**

14   **nerve to ask Steve to this dance. I knew I'd need the**

15   **money to pay for dinner.**

16   **AMY: Pardon, but he should pay. You are taking care of**

17   **everything else.**

18   **AMANDA: Well, he said he was low on cash, so I just said I'd**

19   **take care of it.** *(She picks up phone.)* **Hello?**

20   **HEATHER: I hope David isn't laboring under the incorrect**

21   **assumption that I am picking up this tab.**

22   **AMY: Kevin either.**

23   **AMANDA:** *(Into the phone)* **Oh, sure. No problem. No, really, I**

24   **understand. Hey, really, it's no big deal. What?**

25   **Oh . . . yeah, I guess so.** *(A weak laugh)* **I hope it fits. No,**

26   **you don't have to. It's my pleasure. Yeah. See you at**

27   **school.** *(She hangs up and crosses to the pirate outfits and begins*

28   *folding them, not saying anything.)*

29   **AMY: Amanda, who was that?**

30   **AMANDA: Just Steve. He can't go to the dance.**

31   **HEATHER: Why? What happened?**

32   **AMANDA: Nothing, he just can't go.**

33   **HEATHER: Oh, Amanda, I'm so sorry. Is he all right?**

34   **AMANDA: He's fine. Fine.**

35   **AMY: Are you?**

1   AMANDA: Sure. I'm OK.
2   AMY: What'd he say?
3   AMANDA: He said he hoped I didn't mind.
4   AMY: Mind what? I mean if he's sick or something, it can't
5   be helped, right?
6   AMANDA: He's not sick. He changed his mind.
7   HEATHER: Excuse me? He did what?
8   AMANDA: He said he changed his mind, and he hoped I
9   didn't mind.
10   AMY: And that's OK with you?
11   AMANDA: Well, what am I going to say? "Yes, I mind, dammit!
12   You better go with me to this dance!"
13   HEATHER: The nerve! I can't believe this.
14   AMY: This really screws up our plans. So, he's just going to
15   stay at home or what?
16   AMANDA: No . . . he's taking April instead.
17   HEATHER: *What?!*
18   AMY: He's doing *what?!*
19   AMANDA: He said that April asked him today and that he
20   thought that he and his friends would have a really good
21   time together if April came and that he hoped it was OK
22   with me.
23   AMY: And is it?
24   AMANDA: Well, no, not really. Here. *(She hands AMY the*
25   *costumes she made.)*
26   AMY: What are these for?
27   AMANDA: Well, he said that he needs them for him and April
28   to wear to the dance because it's so late that they don't
29   have time to get anything together. And since April and
30   I are about the same size, he asked. And I said yes.
31   HEATHER: *Omigod! Omigod! Omigod!*
32   AMY: I cannot believe this. This is too much.
33   HEATHER: He actually wants these costumes?
34   AMANDA: You will probably want the hats, too.
35   HEATHER: Why?

1   AMANDA: Well, because you guys are all going together just
2   like it was planned. Everything's the same . . . except I'm
3   not going. April is.
4   HEATHER: I can't believe you are so calm.
5   AMY: I'd be nuts. I can't believe the nerve of him. He actually
6   expects us to still triple with him and April after he burns
7   our best friend.
8   AMANDA: Don't worry about it, OK? I'm fine.
9   HEATHER: Omigod, omigod, omigod!
10   AMY: I'm not fine. I'm going to kill him.
11   AMANDA: It's no big deal.
12   HEATHER: Omigod, omigod!
13   AMY: What do you mean, "No big deal"? This guy is the
14   biggest jerk.
15   HEATHER: Omigod!
16   AMANDA: Will you stop saying that, please?
17   HEATHER: How can you just stand there and be so calm?
18   This is the most unbelievable thing I have ever heard of.
19   The *nerve* of this guy.
20   AMANDA: Hey, two minutes ago he was a big sweetie. David
21   and Kevin's best friend. Now he's a jerk?
22   HEATHER: Omigod, you are being so nice about this.
23   AMY: I'd want to kill him if I were you. I'm *not you and I want*
24   *to kill him.*
25   AMANDA: *(Picking up the hats and handing them to AMY)* **Really,**
26   **I'll get over it.** *(There is a moment of silence while she looks*
27   *at the hats. AMY and HEATHER watch her with pity mixed*
28   *with trepidation. Suddenly she throws them across the room.)*
29   **What an ass!**
30   AMY: All right! She's alive.
31   AMANDA: *(Mimicking STEVE)* **Oh, Amanda, I hope you don't**
32   **mind.** *(Back to her own voice)* **Don't mind? Heck no. And,**
33   **while you're at it, please take the outfits I made for us**
34   **and give them to that other girl you plan to take who's**
35   **better than me. Hey, I'll even drive you there and wait in**

1   the car. By all means, have a great time.

2   HEATHER: Omigod! He didn't ask you to do that, did he?

3   AMANDA: No, but I'm surprised he didn't. *Ooohhh.* I can't

4   believe I just sat there and let him do this to me. *(To AMY)*

5   I need a date. And I need one now. *(Taking back the outfits)*

6   There is no way I am going to sit home while he takes

7   some other girl to this dance in pirate outfits I slaved

8   hours over. I will see him dead first. I may see him dead

9   anyway, just for the fun of it.

10   AMY: OK, give me that phone. My cousin will take you.

11   HEATHER: Dion?

12   AMY: Yes. *(She dials.)*

13   HEATHER: Oooh, he's gorgeous.

14   AMANDA: Even better. I don't care that I don't know him. I

15   don't care that I am getting set up on a pity date. I only

16   care that he's male and available for that dance Saturday

17   night.

18   HEATHER: Steve and April can double with someone else.

19   There is no way we will go with them.

20   AMY: *(Getting off the phone)* It's all set. He's free Saturday

21   night, so he said he'd go.

22   AMANDA: Great. I have an idea. Give me that phone.

23   HEATHER: Who are you calling?

24   AMANDA: April. *(She dials.)*

25   AMY: Why?

26   AMANDA: There is no way she ... Hello, April? ... This is

27   Amanda. I heard you asked Steve to Girl Date ... uh-

28   huh ... Well, guess what? I asked him too ... uh-huh.

29   HEATHER: What are you doing?

30   AMY: I can't believe this.

31   HEATHER: She's a cool one, all right!

32   AMANDA: Well, April, I think you should know what kind of

33   guy Steve is ... You think so? I thought I knew him too. But I

34   had asked him to go with me to Girl Date ... Yes, he

35   did ... Oh, he just called me and said that you ... Uh-huh ...

1   The pirate outfits he said he had? . . . I made them . . . Oh,
2   yeah . . . I thought you'd feel this way . . . No, no, no, I am
3   not going with him . . . You aren't now either? . . . Hey,
4   why not ask Ted . . . No, I think my mom will let him off
5   restriction if she knows the details . . . Sure, don't worry
6   about it . . . You can join our group . . . Outfits? Just go to
7   Wal-Mart and pick up some striped shirts, sailor hats and
8   cut off some jeans at the knees, and you'll fit right
9   in . . . OK, good talking to you, too . . . I figured you didn't
10   know the details. OK, we'll see you later. *(She hangs up.)*
11   Well, my work is done here.
12   AMY: You are so sly.
13   HEATHER: I thought you were going to just lie there like a
14   doormat and take this. But this, this is the ultimate. So,
15   April is going with Ted, you're going with Dion, and Steve
16   is dateless.
17   AMY: If I had my way, that's not all he'd be less.
18   AMANDA: If I can arrange that, I will.
19   HEATHER: We can only hope!
20   AMANDA: *(After a moment's thought, shouts almost in a release of*
21   *frustration.)* **What an ass!** *(And then, quietly, sadly)* **What an**
22   **ass.** *(HEATHER and AMY simply nod in agreement, unable to*
23   *add anything to this observation, as the lights slowly fade.)*
24
25
26
27
28
29
30
31
32
33
34
35

1   # MEN ARE SLIME

2

3   *NICOLE:*   A victim of a horrible date.

4   *STACY:*   A rationalizer, but honest.

5   *PATTY:*   A clever gossip.

6   *SETTING:*   STACY and PATTY are together on-stage, obviously

7   spending the night together; cokes, chips, curlers and nail polish

8   are in evidence.

9

10   NICOLE: Patty? Stacy?

11   STACY: We're in here. *(To PATTY)* **What is she doing here?**

12   PATTY: I thought she had a hot date tonight.

13   NICOLE: *(As she enters)* **Men are slime.**

14   STACY: *(To PATTY)* **She just discovered this?**

15   PATTY: Apparently.

16   NICOLE: I'm serious, girls. Men are slime. The lowest life

17   form known to science. Lower than gutter scum. Rats in

18   the sewer wipe men off of their little rat paws.

19   PATTY: Nicole, may we assume your date this evening was

20   not the success you had originally hoped for?

21   NICOLE: Success? Success is rice. Dating is hell.

22   STACY: You'll get no argument here.

23   PATTY: Stacy told you not to go out on that date, I told you

24   not to go out on that date. But would you listen? No, not

25   you.

26   NICOLE: But he seemed like such a nice guy.

27   STACY: Shopping is nice. Dates should be fabulous . . . as

28   should men.

29   PATTY: But, unfortunately, they are slime.

30   NICOLE: You should have seen. It was not to be believed.

31   STACY: Tell us everything.

32   PATTY: Leave out nothing.

33   NICOLE: You won't believe it. I was there, and I don't believe it.

34   STACY: So, start from the beginning.

35   NICOLE: Well, you know how he said that money was no

1   object, that I should pick out anywhere I wanted to go?

2   **PATTY:** Your first clue. No guy says money is no object

3   without having an object in mind ... if you get my

4   meaning.

5   **NICOLE:** So I say I would love to see that new musical

6   playing at the Performing Arts Center.

7   **STACY:** He took you to see "Friday the Thirteenth," part

8   ten thousand, right?

9   **NICOLE:** Oh, no. He took me to see the musical ... however

10   we were sitting in the nosebleed section. I mean, we were

11   so high pigeons were resting on my shoulders.

12   **STACY:** Give the guy the benefit of the doubt. He probably

13   couldn't get better seats.

14   **NICOLE:** Stacy, for one thing, he said money was no object.

15   For another, we were the *only ones* sitting there. It was

16   embarrassing.

17   **STACY:** Ah. So, what else?

18   **NICOLE:** Next is intermission. He asks me if I would like

19   something to drink. Sure, I say. Guess what he did?

20   **PATTY:** Come back with water.

21   **NICOLE:** Oh, no, nothing as classy as that. He leads me over

22   to the water fountain. *Leads me!*

23   **PATTY:** At least he escorted you.

24   **NICOLE:** He's slime.

25   **STACY:** Nicole, come on. So you sat in the cheap seats and

26   had a sip or two of water instead of a Dr. Pepper. Big deal.

27   **NICOLE:** Oh, but there's more.

28   **PATTY:** Uh, oh.

29   **NICOLE:** After the show he says, "Let's go for a drive." Now

30   I'm thinking, "OK, he doesn't have much money, but

31   maybe we'll talk and he'll turn out to be nice."

32   **STACY:** *(To PATTY)* I lay odds she was wrong on that one.

33   **NICOLE:** Smart girl. He takes me ... are you ready ... ? To

34   Turnbull Canyon Road.

35   **STACY:** No way!

1	PATTY:	On your first date?
2	NICOLE:	I told you. He's a pig.
3	PATTY:	I hope you told him to turn that car right around.
4	NICOLE:	No, I'm an idiot. I thought, give him a try. He's
5		probably going to be nice.
6	STACY:	You were right the first time. You're an idiot.
7	PATTY:	So, what happened? You didn't make out with him
8		did you?
9	NICOLE:	Not that he didn't try.
10	PATTY:	I can't believe it. What a dirt bag.
11	STACY:	How low can you get.
12	NICOLE:	Low? I will tell you how low. So, we're sitting in the
13		car. He's talking about getting to know me *intimately* and
14		I'm trying to remember where the nearest pay phone is.
15		Then all of a sudden he grabs me and tries to kiss me.
16	PATTY:	And . . .
17	STACY:	You didn't kiss him back did you?
18	NICOLE:	*No way!* I told him that I didn't do that sort of thing
19		on the first date. And you know what he did?
20	STACY:	*(A little fright in her voice)* He didn't hurt you, did he?
21	PATTY:	Say the word, and I'll call the cops now.
22	NICOLE:	No, no. Nothing physical. *(She pauses for dramatic*
23		*effect.)* He laughed.
24	STACY:	Laughed? What do you mean, he laughed?
25	NICOLE:	Ha, ha, ha . . . laughed in that sarcastic snooty tone.
26		And then he said . . . "Every girl does."
27	PATTY:	Not this girl.
28	STACY:	This one either.
29	NICOLE:	That's what I told him. I said I didn't and neither
30		did my friends.
31	PATTY:	Good for you.
32	STACY:	What did the filth ball have to say to that?
33	NICOLE:	He asked me if I was a virgin.
34	STACY:	And you said . . . ?
35	NICOLE:	What do you think? I told him yes I was a virgin.

1   **PATTY:**   And proud of it.

2   **NICOLE:**   Damn right.

3   **PATTY:**   Well, good for you. That probably shut him up.

4   **NICOLE:**   You'd like to think it would, wouldn't you?

5   **STACY:**   What did he do then?

6   **NICOLE:**   You know, I was there, in the car, and I don't
7   believe it still.

8   **STACY:**   What?

9   **NICOLE:**   He rolled down the window and then yelled ...

10   **PATTY:**   A scream of frustration, no doubt.

11   **NICOLE:**   No. Nothing quite as civilized as that. He rolled
12   down the window and screamed ... *(She yells.)* *"Nicole*
13   *Kaufman is still a virgin!"*

14   **PATTY:**   You're kidding?

15   **STACY:**   He didn't.

16   **NICOLE:**   Not much he didn't. Can you believe it? He screams
17   it to the entire world.

18   **STACY:**   What a piece of filthy raggedy snot-encrusted debris.

19   **NICOLE:**   And here is the dumbest part. I was embarrassed
20   to have it said. Why? Why should I be embarrassed? He's
21   the one who is a complete fool.

22   **PATTY:**   What a foul piece of dirt.

23   **STACY:**   You shouldn't be embarrassed. You should be proud.

24   **PATTY:**   What did you do?

25   **NICOLE:**   I told him to start that car and take me here. He
26   thought I was kidding. "The night is young," he says.

27   **STACY:**   So is he, at least mentally.

28   **NICOLE:**   So, here I am. Here with my friends, people who
29   care about me. Sensitive, warm, loving people. Bosom
30   companions who will help me plot my revenge against
31   this pig of the forest.

32   **STACY:**   Operation "Men Are Slime."

33   **PATTY:**   We've got all night, Nicole. We'll think of something
34   to exact revenge against this dirt bag.

35   **NICOLE:**   I knew I could count on you two. I'll call my mom,

1 tell her I'm spending the night here and then we will
2 consider all angles.
3 **STACY:** He's a dead man.
4 **PATTY:** *(After a pause)* I heard he was gay.
5 **STACY:** You did? Where? From who?
6 **PATTY:** Here . . . from me.
7 **NICOLE:** Oh, yes. I like that. Gossip. That's a good start.
8 **STACY:** And the night is young. *(The three smile evilly, women*
9 *scorned, and exit laughing in a nasty tone, almost rubbing their*
10 *hands together.)*
11
12
13
14
15
16
17
18
19
20
21
22
23
24
25
26
27
28
29
30
31
32
33
34
35

1 # THINGS CHANGE
2
3 ***PAM:*** A social climber.
4 ***KIM:*** Her former friend.
5 ***SHERRY:*** Friend of both, caught in between.
6 ***SETTING:*** KIM is looking through the movie section of a news-
7 paper in SHERRY's room while SHERRY busies herself getting
8 ready to go out for the evening.
9
10 **KIM:** **Sherry, did you want to go to a movie tonight or what?**
11 **SHERRY:** **I don't know. What's playing?**
12 **KIM:** **The new "Nightmare on Elm Street" is playing at the**
13 **mall. Oooh, and even better, it's a double feature with**
14 **"Friday the Thirteenth," part . . .**
15 **SHERRY:** **One thousand?** *(They laugh.)* **I don't know, Kim.**
16 **Why don't we wait until Pam gets here and then decide**
17 **what we're going to do.**
18 **KIM:** **Pam's coming?**
19 **SHERRY:** **Yeah.**
20 **KIM:** **Oh.**
21 **SHERRY:** **Is that a problem?**
22 **KIM:** **No, no. Really. It's just that I thought she was grounded**
23 **or something.**
24 **SHERRY:** **She was, but it ended today at noon, so she's**
25 **coming over here to celebrate.**
26 **KIM:** **Does she know I'm here?**
27 **SHERRY:** **I told her you would be. Why? Is there a problem**
28 **with you two?**
29 **KIM:** **No. Not at all.** *(She refers back to the movie section.)* **I'll**
30 **check the starting times.**
31 **PAM:** *(Entering)* **Starting times for what?**
32 **SHERRY:** **Pam! You're a free woman! Welcome back to**
33 **liberation.**
34 **PAM:** **I'm here, I'm happy. I am ready to *par-tee!***
35 **KIM:** **I was just checking the movie schedule.**

1   **PAM:**   **I'm sure you were, dear, but I said party, not movie.**

2   **KIM:**   **Well, Sherry and I had agreed to see a movie.**

3   **SHERRY:**   **Well, Kim, not really. We just talked about it.**

4   **KIM:**   **But I thought you wanted to see "Friday the Thirteenth"**

5   **and "Nightmare on Elm Street."**

6   **PAM:**   **Isn't that just a bit dull for a Saturday night?**

7   **KIM:**   **I don't think so.**

8   **PAM:**   *(Under her breath)* **You wouldn't.**

9   **SHERRY:**   *(After a moment of uncomfortable silence)* **Hey, I'm sure**

10   **there's something we could do that we'd all like.**

11   **PAM:**   **It's a great night, there's got to be a party somewhere.**

12   **Let's just hit the streets and start walking.**

13   **KIM:**   *(Looking directly at Pam)* **Yes, it's a lovely night for street**

14   **walking.**

15   **PAM:**   *(With venom)* **Excuse me?**

16   **SHERRY:**   *(Rushing to save the situation)* **I've got the car tonight.**

17   **I'll drive.**

18   **KIM and PAM:**   **Shotgun!** *(They glare at each other.)*

19   **KIM:**   **I called it first.**

20   **PAM:**   **I'm just sure, Kim. We called it at the same time.**

21   **KIM:**   **I called it before you even got here.**

22   **PAM:**   **You didn't even know I was coming.**

23   **KIM:**   **So, I get it by default. You weren't *supposed* to be here**

24   **tonight.**

25   **PAM:**   **Who says?**

26   **SHERRY:**   **What is going on here?**

27   **KIM:**   **Nothing.**

28   **PAM:**   **Kim is just being her usual obnoxious self.**

29   **KIM:**   **What does *that* mean?**

30   **PAM:**   **Look it up.**

31   **SHERRY:**   **It means rude and . . .**

32   **KIM:**   **I *know* what it means.** *(Right at PAM)* **But what does she**

33   **mean by it?**

34   **PAM:**   **Nothing.**

35   **SHERRY:**   **She doesn't mean anything, Kim. She was just**

1	trying to be funny.
2	PAM: That's right. You just have no sense of humor.
3	SHERRY: Well, sometimes you're not very funny, Pam.
4	KIM: Thank you. I'm glad to see you're on my side.
5	PAM: Are you on her side, Sherry?
6	KIM: Things were fine until you got here and screwed up the
7	plans.
8	PAM: Oh, yeah, great plans. I know I would love to spend my
9	Saturday evening out at a movie with two girls.
10	KIM: Hey, if it is that much of a drag, don't.
11	PAM: Maybe I won't.
12	SHERRY: Kim, Gary is having a party, you know.
13	KIM: No, I didn't know.
14	PAM: Maybe you weren't invited.
15	KIM: Maybe not, so who cares?
16	PAM: Obviously you do.
17	SHERRY: There are no invitations and you both know that.
18	It's just a party. You just go.
19	KIM: I don't even like Gary.
20	PAM: Then don't go.
21	KIM: I have no intention of going. Sherry and I made plans
22	for the night to see movies and that's what we're going
23	to do, right, Sherry?
24	SHERRY: I'd kinda like to go to Gary's party.
25	KIM: Oh, fine. Well, you two just have a great time, OK?
26	PAM: We will.
27	SHERRY: Kim, you can come, too, you know.
28	KIM: No, I can't. I don't like those people. They are all so
29	phony.
30	SHERRY: No they're not. They just like to have fun.
31	KIM: Yeah, at everyone's expense but their own. All they do
32	is sit around and drink and then rag on everbody who
33	they think isn't as cool as them.
34	PAM: Like you?
35	SHERRY: Pam . . .

1	KIM:	No, she's right. I'm not "as cool as them," and I don't
2		want to be. They act like a bunch of losers.
3	PAM:	They're the most popular kids at school.
4	KIM:	Big deal. I'm not impressed.
5	PAM:	No, you're not included. Come on, Sherry.
6	SHERRY:	Pam, what's with you lately?
7	KIM:	She's been like this since school started.
8	PAM:	Like what?
9	KIM:	Bitchy, stuck up, "cool."
10	PAM:	Kim, face it. I have been accepted at this school by
11		people you can only dream about being friends with.
12	SHERRY:	I don't understand this. We three have been
13		friends since seventh grade. What is this? We hit high
14		school and now, poof, it's gone?
15	PAM:	We're just going in different directions. I choose to go
16		up in the social world, while Kim chooses to make that
17		downward slide into the land of the dorks.
18	KIM:	I can't believe we were ever best friends.
19	PAM:	I feel the same way.
20	SHERRY:	I don't. Come on, you two. Be nice and let's go out.
21	KIM:	No, I think I'll just go home. Pam certainly makes it
22		clear that I am not welcome and it's evident that you
23		want to go to Gary's party, so I'll just see you around.
24	SHERRY:	Kim, don't leave.
25	PAM:	Sherry, it's her decision.
26	KIM:	Call me tomorrow, if you want.
27	SHERRY:	Are you sure you don't want to go?
28	KIM:	*(Looking directly at PAM, who stares back)* **Absolutely.**
29	SHERRY:	I'll call you, OK?
30	KIM:	*(Leaving)* OK. See ya.
31	PAM:	What a loser.
32	SHERRY:	Shut up, Pam.
33	PAM:	What's your problem?
34	SHERRY:	Nothing. If we're going, let's go. *(She exits.)*
35	PAM:	Sheesh, what's wrong with you?

1   **SHERRY:**   *(As she exits)* **Just shut up and get in the car.**
2   **PAM:**   **Fine, I'm coming.** *(Mumbling nastily to herself)* **This is**
3   **going to be a great evening, I can tell.** *(Out loud)* **I'll be**
4   **right there.**
5
6
7
8
9
10
11
12
13
14
15
16
17
18
19
20
21
22
23
24
25
26
27
28
29
30
31
32
33
34
35

1   # ROAD TRIPS
2
3   *HEATHER:*   Age 17.
4   *LAURIE:*   Age 16.
5   *CHANDRA:*   Age 17.
6   *TAMARA:*   Age 16.
7   *SETTING:*   The scene takes place in and around a car. The car can
8   be represented by the use of five chairs, two in the front to
9   represent the front seat and three in back to simulate a back
10   seat. The four girls enter, each carrying her own pack of supplies.
11
12   HEATHER: I get shotgun.
13   LAURIE: Why you?
14   HEATHER: 'Cause I get car sick.
15   CHANDRA: I don't care where anybody sits. I just want to get
16   started.
17   TAMARA: I'll drive.
18   ALL THREE: *No!*
19   TAMARA: Sheesh.
20   LAURIE: Well, Tamara, you can't blame us
21   CHANDRA: Really. You are a terrible driver!
22   TAMARA: I'm not!
23   HEATHER: Who else but you took her driving test five times
24   before she finally passed?
25   LAURIE: And I think that was a pity pass, too. The guy just
26   felt sorry for you sitting there crying hysterically.
27   CHANDRA: He probably was afraid he'd get stuck with her if
28   she took the test again.
29   HEATHER: There is no way you are driving. *(She takes the*
30   *keys from TAMARA.)*
31   TAMARA: But it's my car!
32   LAURIE: Tough, get in the back.
33   TAMARA: This just isn't fair.
34   CHANDRA: So, who wants to drive?
35   HEATHER: I will.

1 LAURIE: Someone guard her and make sure she doesn't lock
2   the keys in the car.
3 CHANDRA: I have a spare in my pocket.
4 TAMARA: Why do *you* have a spare key to *my* car?
5 CHANDRA: Your mom gave it to me.
6 TAMARA: Does no one trust me?
7 ALL THREE: No!
8 TAMARA: Sheesh!
9 LAURIE: Heather, I'll sit in the back for the first part of the
10   trip, but I don't want to be back there forever. If I go too
11   long without seeing something other than the back of
12   your head I'll get sick, too.
13 HEATHER: Excuse me?
14 LAURIE: No, I don't mean your head makes me sick. If I can't
15   see, I get sick. Never mind.
16 CHANDRA: Get in the car everyone.
17 TAMARA: *(Settling in the back seat)* I can't believe we are using
18   my car and you won't let me drive.
19 CHANDRA: Is everyone ready? *(Various affirmations)* Does
20   everyone have everything they need? *(They all check their*
21   *own bags, and again various affirmations.)* Then we're off!
22   *(She starts the "car" and they begin their trip.)* Heather, look
23   at the map. How far is it to the lake?
24 HEATHER: *(Looking at a map)* According to this, about ninety
25   miles.
26 CHANDRA: That should take us about an hour and a half,
27   maybe longer.
28 TAMARA: I've been there before. It didn't take that long
29   when I drove.
30 LAURIE: Why are we not surprised?
31 CHANDRA: Now, we've got almost two hours. What should
32   we talk about?
33 HEATHER: The dance?
34 TAMARA: Did you see Brandon with Elizabeth? Sickening or
35   what?

73

1   LAURIE: No kidding. I was ready to chip in and get them a
2   room.
3   HEATHER: Some people just have no ...
4   CHANDRA: Wait a minute. Wait a minute. We've got a long
5   drive. Why don't we use this time to talk about something
6   other than guys or dances or gossip?
7   TAMARA: Why?
8   CHANDRA: Because, that same old stuff gets boring. There's
9   more to our lives than guys and gossip, isn't there?
10   LAURIE: I would hope so.
11   HEATHER: OK, then what should we talk about? *(They sit in*
12   *thoughtful silence.)*
13   TAMARA: Uh, I was reading in the paper where ...
14   CHANDRA: Wait a minute, you were reading the paper?
15   TAMARA: You don't have to sound so surprised.
16   HEATHER: She doesn't have to. It came naturally.
17   LAURIE: Let her talk, guys. This should be interesting if
18   nothing else.
19   TAMARA: Thank you, Laurie. Anyway, I was reading that a
20   single woman over thirty-five years old has more of a
21   chance getting shot by a terrorist than finding a husband.
22   HEATHER: What?
23   TAMARA: I'm serious! It was in the paper.
24   LAURIE: Which one, the *National Enquirer*?
25   CHANDRA: No, she's right. I read that, too. It was in the *L. A.*
26   *Times.*
27   LAURIE: No kidding. Wow. A terrorist, huh?
28   HEATHER: That's just ridiculous. It's just more rhetoric
29   from uptight men who want to keep women down.
30   LAURIE: That's probably true. Men are ...
31   TAMARA: Wait a minute! Chandra says she saw it, so now we
32   all believe it was in the paper and we can discuss it? How
33   come no one believed me when I brought it up?
34   LAURIE: Well, face it, Tamara. You aren't exactly the most
35   well-versed on current affairs.

1 **TAMARA:** *(Diving into her bag and pulling out a candy bar and*
2 *coke)* **Fine. I'll just sit here and eat. You guys talk without**
3 **me.** *(She opens the can and drinks it down.)*
4 **CHANDRA:** *(Rolling her eyes)* **Tamara, I'm sorry.** *(She looks in*
5 *rearview mirror and sees TAMARA looking at her.)* **No, really,**
6 **I am.**
7 **TAMARA:** **I'm not stupid, you know.**
8 **LAURIE:** **Sorry, Tamara.**
9 **HEATHER:** **Me, too.** *(They sit for a while, uncomfortable in the*
10 *silence, the lights fade a bit to indicate time passing.)*
11 **TAMARA:** *(As a way of getting past the moment)* **Does anyone**
12 **else want a coke?**
13 **CHANDRA:** **Yeah, pass one up.**
14 **HEATHER:** **Yeah, I'll take one.**
15 **TAMARA:** **Laurie?**
16 **LAURIE:** **Sure. Hey, anyone want some bread sticks? Fat**
17 **free!**
18 **CHANDRA:** **Yep!**
19 **HEATHER:** **Pull over. You eat, I'll drive.**
20 **CHANDRA:** **OK.**
21 **LAURIE:** **Shotgun!**
22 **TAMARA:** **No, me!**
23 **LAURIE:** **I told you if I sit in the back too long, I'll get sick.**
24 **TAMARA:** **Jeez, it's my car! I'm driving.**
25 **CHANDRA:** **No way!**
26 **TAMARA:** **Yes way. Give me the keys!**
27 **HEATHER:** **I swear Tamara, if you get us in an accident, I**
28 **will kill you.**
29 **TAMARA:** **Just give me the keys.**
30 **LAURIE:** **You better be careful.**
31 **CHANDRA:** *(Reluctantly handing over the keys)* **I just know we**
32 **are all going to regret this.**
33 **TAMARA:** **OK, everybody in and let's go.** *(She puts the keys in*
34 *and starts the car.)* **Wait!** *(The girls all look up, startled.)* **I have**
35 **to finish my drink.**

1   LAURIE: You have the bladder of a camel. Isn't that the
2   fourth coke you've had today?
3   TAMARA: Don't know, don't care.
4   HEATHER: How much longer?
5   CHANDRA: *(Referring to the map and looking out the window for*
6   *landmarks)* **According to this, we've gone about forty**
7   miles.
8   TAMARA: Nothing looks familiar.
9   LAURIE: That's because when you come here you go so fast
10   it's all a blur.
11   HEATHER: Are you sure we're going the right way?
12   CHANDRA: I just followed the map that was in here. If you
13   take the next road, we should be OK.
14   TAMARA: Well, as they say on the Peter Pan ride, "Here we
15   goooo."
16   LAURIE: We're doomed.
17   HEATHER: Chandra, toss me some cookies.
18   CHANDRA: Speaking of tossing cookies, take a look at the
19   outfit the girl in the next car is wearing.
20   LAURIE: Oh, brother. *(Very catty)* Girls, do we like that?
21   ALL FOUR: I don't *think* so.
22   HEATHER: Roll down the window and ask her if that huge
23   yellow bow is all the rage back in Mayberry.
24   TAMARA: Look at the Goober next to her.
25   CHANDRA: *(With buck teeth)* Gee, Clarabell, that's a mighty
26   fine frock ya'll are wearin'.
27   TAMARA: Oh, Festus, you is just too a-dor-a-ble in that perty
28   green cowboy shirt and matching straw hat.
29   CHANDRA and TAMARA: *(A goofy laugh)* Har, har, har.
30   HEATHER: You guys are so mean!
31   CHANDRA: Now, lissen here, missy. Me and my lil' gal is just
32   on our way to the tractor pull ready to have a good ole
33   time.
34   TAMARA: *(Patting LAURIE)* An' our little precious Velvetlee
35   is goin' to find herself a man, inn't that right, Velvetlee?

1   LAURIE: You betcha it is. I'm notta goin' home till I find my
2   own man that dresses just as good as my daddy. *(She rubs*
3   *her hand across her nose.)* **'Cause I'm worth it!**
4   HEATHER: So much for discussing current events.
5   CHANDRA: Fashion is current.
6   LAURIE: Not in that car.
7   TAMARA: I read that . . .
8   HEATHER: You don't really expect us to believe that you
9   read two things, do you?
10   TAMARA: Funny, Heather. Anyway, I read that since most
11   of the women's fashions are designed by men that it is
12   their way of getting back at their mothers for mistreating
13   them when they were boys.
14   HEATHER: That's just stupid.
15   LAURIE: No, I read that article too. It was in *Cosmopolitan.*
16   It said that "fashion is the means by which the male
17   designer takes out his frustration on his mother."
18   CHANDRA: What?
19   LAURIE: Think about it. Men designed high heels for whom?
20   Not men, that's for sure. So, who walks around with
21   aching feet? Women dressed by men.
22   CHANDRA: It's like, all these men who can't get a date sit in
23   some room designing clothes that will ultimately make
24   the woman look at past pictures of herself and cringe in
25   horror.
26   TAMARA: Heather, think about it. What's the worst fashion
27   design that's ever happened to a man? Probably the
28   polyester leisure suit.
29   LAURIE: No, no, no, no, no, no, it's . . . *speedos! (All the girls*
30   *react with varying degrees of horrified laughter.)*
31   CHANDRA: Disgusting!
32   TAMARA: So stupid. Do they really think they look good in
33   those?
34   HEATHER: Give me a man in a pair of fine fitting 501s any
35   day!

1 TAMARA: **Whoa, yeah, baby!** *(Suddenly her eyes open in surprise*
2 *and nervousness.)* **Uh-oh . . . I need to find a bathroom!**
3 LAURIE: **I knew those four cokes would kick in.**
4 CHANDRA: **We're in the middle of nowhere. You have to**
5 **wait at least twenty-five more miles before the nearest**
6 **rest stop.**
7 TAMARA: **Can't. Can't do it. Ain't gonna happen. I'm pulling**
8 **off here.**
9 LAURIE: **What?**
10 HEATHER: **Here? Why?**
11 TAMARA: *(Pulling off, turning off car, leaving)* **Bushes, hide, no**
12 **time to chat.** *(She is gone.)*
13 CHANDRA: **What an idiot. Well, what the heck. We can**
14 **stretch our legs. We should be there pretty soon.**
15 LAURIE: *(Calling off)* **Hurry up, Tamara.**
16 TAMARA: *(Calling back)* **I'm going as fast as I can . . . oh, damn.**
17 HEATHER: **What's wrong?**
18 TAMARA: **Do any of you have any tissues or a hanky or**
19 **something?**
20 CHANDRA: **Omigod.** *(The three girls erupt in laughter.)* **Sorry.**
21 TAMARA: **Oh, fine. Just terrific.**
22 LAURIE: **Only Tamara, you know.**
23 CHANDRA: **No kidding.**
24 HEATHER: **What an idiot.**
25 TAMARA: *(Entering)* **I can't believe in all these supplies we**
26 **have for this picnic we didn't have one tissue or napkin.**
27 HEATHER: **Oops.**
28 TAMARA: **What?**
29 HEATHER: **You only asked for a hanky or tissue.** *(She*
30 *reaches into her bag and pulls out a pile of napkins.)* **Sorry.**
31 LAURIE: **What'd you use?**
32 TAMARA: **Leaves. Probably disease infested leaves. I'll never**
33 **look at a tree the same way again. OK, enough laughing**
34 **at me. Let's go.** *(The girls get back in the car, and TAMARA*
35 *attempts to start it.)* **Uh-oh.**

1   CHANDRA: Uh-oh?

2   TAMARA: It's nothing. *(She tries again.)* Uh-oh.

3   HEATHER: I *knew* it! This car hates you. It *knew* you were
4   driving and it's punishing all of us.

5   TAMARA: Wait, it will start. *(Again, nothing)*

6   LAURIE: We're going to miss this picnic, aren't we? This is
7   just so typical of anything we four do. Something always
8   gets screwed up.

9   TAMARA: Let's look under the hood. *(They get out of the car,*
10   *pantomime opening the hood.)* Yep, that's an engine all right.

11 CHANDRA: Why are we even looking? None of us know
12   jack about cars.

13 LAURIE: My father was always trying to teach me. Would I
14   listen to him? *Nooo*, not me. So now we are stuck here.
15   Not a phone, not a call box, nothing. *(She flops on the*
16   *ground.)* Great! Give me one of those sandwiches.

17 CHANDRA: *(Going to her bag of stuff, she pulls out a sandwich*
18   *and tosses it to LAURIE.)* Here. Anyone else?

19 HEATHER: Yeah, I'll take one. It will probably be our last
20   meal. Someone will find us days from now, dead,
21   clutching the remains of bread crusts in our cold inert
22   hands.

23 LAURIE: *(Picking up HEATHER's train of thought)* Maggots
24   crawling on our carcasses, feasting on what is left after
25   the coyotes get through with us.

26 CHANDRA: *(Continuing)* Crows playing games with what
27   look like marbles but in actuality were once our eyes. All
28   because we let Tamara drive and kill the car. *(They all*
29   *throw her dirty looks.)*

30 TAMARA: It's not my fault! This car does hate me. And I hate
31   it. *Stupid car! (She hits it.)*

32 CHANDRA: *(Sitting in the driver's seat)* Oh, good, Tamara,
33   really tick it off. *(She leans back, and then notices something.)*
34   Tamara . . . ?

35 TAMARA: What?

79

1 CHANDRA: When you left to relieve yourself, did you turn
2 the car off?
3 TAMARA: Of course. You don't hear the engine do you?
4 CHANDRA: Did you put the gearshift in park?
5 TAMARA: I don't know. The brake's on, isn't it?
6 CHANDRA: Uh-huh.
7 TAMARA: Then why should I put it in park? It's not going
8 anywhere.
9 HEATHER: What an idiot.
10 TAMARA: What?
11 CHANDRA: You tried to start the car in drive.
12 TAMARA: So?
13 LAURIE: A car has to be in neutral or park or it won't start.
14 TAMARA: I'm not a mechanic. How am I supposed to know
15 that?
16 LAURIE: Everybody knows that.
17 CHANDRA: *(Putting the keys in and turning the ignition)* **We have**
18 **power, ladies.** *(Excited and relieved responses)* **Back in and**
19 **let's go.**
20 TAMARA: Move over, Chandra.
21 CHANDRA: Think again.
22 HEATHER: Tamara, we want to get there, OK? Just sit back
23 here and try not to let the car know you're in it.
24 TAMARA: This is *not* fair.
25 LAURIE: Listen, Tamara, just get in this stinkin' car and be
26 quiet. So far this has not been one of our better days
27 together.
28 TAMARA: It's not my fault the car wouldn't start. *(The girls*
29 *give her looks of amazement.)* **OK, maybe it was. Fine,**
30 **Chandra, you drive.**
31 CHANDRA: Thank you. *(The girls settle in.)* **Are we ready?**
32 TAMARA: *Wait!* I need another drink.
33 HEATHER: No way. Not another liquid in you till we get to
34 the lake.
35 TAMARA: This is *not* fair.

1   **LAURIE:**   Too bad.
2   **TAMARA:**   I read that if you go too long without liquid . . .
3   **CHANDRA:**   Someone shove an Oreo in her mouth, please.
4   **HEATHER:**   Next road trip, we take my car.
5   **TAMARA:**   *(Through the chewing of the Oreo)* **Shotgun!**
6
7
8
9
10
11
12
13
14
15
16
17
18
19
20
21
22
23
24
25
26
27
28
29
30
31
32
33
34
35

CHURCH

NICOLE: A Catholic girl.

JENNY: A Protestant girl.

SHELLY: A Catholic girl.

LORI: A Jewish girl.

CORI: A Protestant girl.

SETTING: Five girls, all about seventeen, enter a church. They are nervous and looking around as if they shouldn't be in there . . . which they shouldn't.

NICOLE: Shhh. Come on. And be quiet.

JENNY: Well, this is about the dumbest thing we have ever done.

SHELLY: Shhh. If we get caught, there is no way to explain this without looking like fools.

LORI: Personally, I find this very offensive. Cutting class and spending the time in church. What, we couldn't go to the synagogue?

CORI: This is blasphemous. I know God is going to punish us.

LORI: He won't punish me. I'm not Catholic.

NICOLE: Yeah, yeah, you're one of the "chosen people." We've all heard it before.

JENNY: Omigod. *(They all look at her, she quickly looks up to the heavens.)* Just kidding. This is so evil.

SHELLY: Evil? No, just dumb. I can't believe we sneak out of school and come here. What's the point? So we can go to confession and feel like we've gotten rid of our sin of cutting school?

LORI: I'm not going into any box and spilling my guts, thank you very much.

CORI: Lori, just be quiet. Now, everybody, sit down.

JENNY: I want to look around. I've never been in a Catholic church before. *(She starts to wander toward the altar.)*

NICOLE: *Stop!* *(They all freeze.)* Have you lost your mind?

1   **JENNY:**   **What? What?**

2   **NICOLE:**   **You can't go on the altar for heaven's sake.**

3   **SHELLY:**   **Don't you know anything?**

4   **CORI:**   **Why not?**

5   **NICOLE:**   **I guess Shelly and I are the only two Catholics in**

6   **the crowd.**

7   **SHELLY:**   **I guess so. Only priests can go on the altar.**

8   **LORI:**   **Only priests?**

9   **JENNY:**   **Why?**

10   **SHELLY:**   **Because. That's just the way it is.**

11   **CORI:**   **Wait a minute. I just thought of something. Only men**

12   **are priests in the Catholic church, huh?**

13   **NICOLE:**   **Yes. Women are nuns.**

14   **LORI:**   **So, only men are allowed on the altar?**

15   **SHELLY:**   **Yeah.**

16   **LORI:**   **I don't *think* so.** *(LORI, JENNY and CORI head for the*

17   *altar.)*

18   **NICOLE:**   *No!*

19   **SHELLY:**   *Stop!*

20   **JENNY:**   **Why?**

21   **CORI:**   **We're not Catholic, we won't burn in hell.**

22   **LORI:**   **We are making a strike for women everywhere.**

23   **NICOLE:**   **Just . . . no. OK?** *(She looks around, as if waiting for*

24   *lightning to strike.)*

25   **SHELLY:**   **Come on, we're being bad enough by using this**

26   **church as our ditching place. Let's not pour salt into the**

27   **wound.**

28   **NICOLE:**   **Really. Just behave, OK?**

29   **CORI:**   **All right. Sheesh. It's not like lightning will strike us**

30   **dead or anything.**

31   **LORI:**   **Besides, the Catholic church is so outdated. I mean,**

32   **really, abstinence is so passé.**

33   **JENNY:**   *(Raising a curious eyebrow)* **Oh, Lori . . . is it?** *(All four*

34   *of the girls lean in, expectantly.)*

35   **LORI:**   **From what I've heard. No personal experience.**

1   CORI: Yeah, right.
2   LORI: It's true.
3   SHELLY: Hmmm. Certainly it is.
4   LORI: Shelly!
5   NICOLE: Lori, Lori, Lori. What have you been hiding from
6   us?
7   JENNY: Tell all, now.
8   LORI: That's enough. I'm leaving if you don't stop.
9   CORI: We're just kidding. Now, everybody sit down and get
10   comfortable. *(The girls sit in various positions on floor or in*
11   *"pews.")*
12   SHELLY: OK, Cori, why are we here?
13   CORI: OK. The way I see it, we are nearing the end of our
14   junior year and now is the time we need to make some
15   sort of decisions about life.
16   JENNY: Now? We've got a whole year left of school.
17   CORI: Jenny, I know that, but it's more than just school. It's
18   us.
19   NICOLE: How so?
20   SHELLY: And why in a church?
21   CORI: The way I figure it, it's the last place anyone would
22   think of looking for us. And face it, this is a very peaceful
23   place. Very holy.
24   LORI: Not for all of us.
25   NICOLE: Lori, she's not asking you to take communion, you
26   know.
27   CORI: Yes, but I am asking you to communicate.
28   JENNY: What? Oh, communicate, communion. Very clever.
29   CORI: Anyway, here we are in this quiet place that is very
30   open to inner reflection.
31   NICOLE: Uh-oh.
32   CORI: What?
33   SHELLY: You're going to get metaphysical on us, aren't you?
34   CORI: Why do you say that? *(She reaches for her purse.)*
35   JENNY: Incense. You're bringing out that damn incense,

1   **aren't you?**
2 **CORI:**   **Maybe.**
3 **LORI:**   **I hate that stuff. It stinks to high heaven.**
4 **SHELLY:**   **Then this is the perfect place, isn't it? Ha!**
5 **NICOLE:**   *(Seeing CORI bring out the incense stick)* **You aren't**
6   **really going to light that, are you?**
7 **CORI:**   **Yes. It will set the appropriate mood.**
8 **SHELLY:**   **Oh, brother.**
9 **CORI:**   **Shelly, trust me.**
10 **SHELLY:**   **Oh, brother.**
11 **CORI:**   **OK, everybody join hands for a moment and feel the**
12   **power of our friendship.** *(They reluctantly come together in*
13   *a circle and join hands.)*
14 **JENNY:**   *(After a moment of this quiet hand holding, begins singing.)*
15   **Kumbah ya, my Lord, Kumbah ya.** *(All the girls break up*
16   *laughing and sit back down.)*
17 **CORI:**   **Nice mood breaker, Jen.**
18 **JENNY:**   **Well, this was just getting too heavy for me.**
19 **NICOLE:**   **I think what Cori is trying to do is really sweet.**
20 **CORI:**   **Do you?**
21 **NICOLE:**   **Yes.**
22 **LORI:**   **Then, would you mind explaining it to me?**
23 **NICOLE:**   **I think she wants us to *bond*.**
24 **SHELLY:**   **Bond?**
25 **NICOLE:**   **Yes. Am I right?**
26 **CORI:**   **Yes. You see, we are at the end of our junior year. We**
27   **have this great friendship and as we enter adulthood . . .**
28 **LORI:**   **Seniors are adults?**
29 **CORI:**   **Almost.**
30 **LORI:**   **News to me.**
31 **CORI:**   **Anyway, I thought we should take this time to really**
32   **strengthen our relationship because who knows where**
33   **we will all be a year from today.**
34 **SHELLY:**   **With any kind of luck, packing and getting the hell**
35   **out of this crummy little town.**

1   CORI: Exactly. We will all be leaving for our new adult lives
2   and I figured if we did this we would all have this one
3   moment we could look back on and cherish forever.
4   NICOLE: I think this is so cool.
5   SHELLY: I think so too.
6   LORI: I don't.
7   JENNY: Why?
8   LORI: Because, it makes it seem like such an ending.
9   CORI: But, don't you see, it's really like a beginning.
10   NICOLE: Yeah. It's like the first time we take that adult road.
11   JENNY: And the best part is that we can do it all together.
12   SHELLY: And here, in this church. Where we have to be
13   honest with each other, otherwise it will be like some
14   sort of sin.
15   LORI: Not to me.
16   NICOLE: Bear with it, OK, Lori?
17   LORI: Oh, all right. But I still think this is a little weird.
18   CORI: OK, who wants to go first?
19   SHELLY: What do you mean, go first?
20   CORI: Start with the bonding experience?
21   NICOLE: I will. What do I do?
22   CORI: OK. First thing is you have to say how you feel about
23   each person in the group. And you have to be honest.
24   JENNY: Oh, God. I don't know if this is such a good idea.
25   CORI: It will be, trust me. Because we have to open ourselves
26   up to constructive criticism. But the main rule is you
27   have to end on a positive note.
28   NICOLE: I'll go last.
29   LORI: You said you'd go first.
30   NICOLE: I changed my mind.
31   CORI: Too late. Go.
32   NICOLE: Rats. OK. How I feel. I guess I will start with the
33   negative stuff, right?
34   CORI: Right.
35   JENNY: And we have to be honest?

1 CORI: That's the whole key.
2 LORI: I'm telling you, I don't know if this is such a good idea.
3 NICOLE: OK, Lori.
4 LORI: I knew she'd start with me. I always get the negative
5   stuff.
6 CORI: Oh, and another thing. You have to sit and listen
7   carefully, but don't judge others for what they say. And
8   you can't go on forever and ever. Just make your points
9   and move on, because otherwise it's boring.
10 SHELLY: Boring?
11 JENNY: I can see that.
12 CORI: You also have to hold this incense stick while you talk.
13 NICOLE: Oh, please, that stuff makes me nauseous.
14 CORI: It's part of the memory bank, though. You see, you
15   have to bring in all the senses.
16 NICOLE: Gimme the damn thing. OK. First, I think the most
17   negative thing I can say is that sometimes we, as friends,
18   aren't completely honest with each other.
19 LORI: What do you mean?
20 SHELLY: Lori, you're not supposed to talk.
21 LORI: Oh. Sorry.
22 NICOLE: What I mean is that sometimes, not always, but
23   sometimes some of us don't always tell the truth about
24   things. Like, for example, me. Shelly, when you asked me
25   if I liked John, I said yes, when really I thought he was
26   a slime ball and would end up hurting you. And I was
27   right. Maybe if I had been honest with you to begin with,
28   you wouldn't have gotten hurt.
29 CORI: See, this is good. Nicole makes an observation and
30   then uses herself as an example.
31 SHELLY: You didn't like John?
32 NICOLE: The man was pond scum. In fact, that comparison is
33   an insult to pond scum.
34 SHELLY: I wish you would have told me then.
35 NICOLE: Would it have really done any good?

1   SHELLY: Probably not.

2   JENNY: OK, the positive stuff.

3   NICOLE: OK. Hmmm. I think the best thing about our
4   friendship is that we can all get together and accept each
5   other for who we are. I mean, we are all so different, but
6   I look around here and I see the best friends I have ever
7   had. And I don't think that I will ever have friends this
8   close again. Ever. I love each one of you. *(They all respond*
9   *with smiles and warm feelings.)*

10   JENNY: My turn, my turn. I really don't have much negative
11   to say, except that something that really bothers me is
12   that sometimes I feel left out.

13   ALL GIRLS: No way, uh-uh. *(Etc.)*

14   JENNY: Hey, I'm being honest. Sometimes I feel, because my
15   parents won't let me do a lot of the things that you guys
16   can do, that you make plans and just don't include me,
17   because I probably can't do them anyway.

18   LORI: Well, then, can you blame us?

19   SHELLY: Lori, don't interrupt!

20   LORI: Sheesh . . . sorry.

21   JENNY: It's just that I would like to be thought of as part of
22   the group all the time, but sometimes I feel sort of left
23   out. Whoa. I can't believe I really said that. I didn't realize
24   how much that had bothered me.

25   SHELLY: We don't mean to make you feel that way.

26   JENNY: I know. It's just that's the way I feel. But, I also feel —
27   now here comes the positive stuff — I feel like you guys
28   are the only people at school who really know who I am.
29   I mean, I have other friends and all, but the four of you
30   are the only people I can tell stuff to that I know won't
31   get blabbed all over the campus. I know that I can be
32   myself with you and you won't judge me or hate me or
33   anything. That I can flip out when I need to and you won't
34   take it personally. That I can be as PMSy as I need to be
35   and don't have to apologize for it later. Oh, God. Cori, I

1   just realized that you're right. I will always remember
2   this moment in time. I am looking in the faces of my very
3   best friends and I will always have this memory. *(She*
4   *begins to tear up.)* **Damn, I don't want to cry.**
5   **LORI:**   If you keep swearing, you won't have to cry, because
6   lightning will strike you dead. OK, my turn!
7   **NICOLE:**   Pass Lori the incense, Jen.
8   **LORI:**   Do I really have to hold that stuff? My sinuses simply
9   can't take it.
10   **JENNY:**   Hey, it's part of the concept. Go with it, OK? *(To the*
11   *others)* **Jeez, she complains a lot!**
12   **CORI:**   Just shut up, take the thing and do it!
13   **LORI:**   Fine. *(She gingerly holds the stick of incense.)* I know
14   right off the first thing I want to say. I hate when all of
15   you always tell me to shut up. It gets really annoying and
16   sometimes it really hurts my feelings. Like now, for
17   instance. I don't mean to talk as much as I do, but
18   sometimes I just can't seem to turn it off. Sometimes, you
19   know, it just gets really tiring to always be told to shut
20   up. Now, my positive comment is that I know I deserve
21   it and you guys are the only people I know who will let
22   me talk on and on, tell me to shut up, and still like me
23   and trust me with your secrets. Because you trust me
24   enough to know that even if I talk and talk, whatever is
25   said in confidence will never be repeated. And I really
26   don't think we know too many people we can say that
27   about. We have something that is truly special. Trust. I
28   absolutely trust all of you and I know that I will always
29   be able to say that no matter where we go or what we
30   do. Oh, wow, this really is gut-spilling time, isn't it? Let
31   me take a big whiff of this stuff so every time I smell this
32   smell, I will remember this. *(To CORI)* **What flavor is this,**
33   anyway?
34   **CORI:**   Beechwood.
35   **LORI:**   Swell. When am I ever going to smell beechwood? I'll

1   **have to go out now and buy a gross of this stuff.** *(She*
2   *passes it to SHELLY.)*
3   SHELLY: **OK, we've had love and acceptance and trust.**
4   **There's nothing else left.**
5   NICOLE: **Come on, Shelly.** *Booonnnddd* **with us.**
6   SHELLY: **Honestly, I can't think of anything negative to say.**
7   NICOLE: **I can understand that.**
8   JENNY: **Hey, she used up all her negativity on John.**
9   SHELLY: **Hey, now. Go easy.**
10 CORI: **Oh, Shelly, please. He treated you like feces.**
11 SHELLY: **It wasn't all him, you know.**
12 NICOLE: **Sure it wasn't. You treated him like a king.**
13 SHELLY: **OK, I know what negative thing I have to say. I get**
14   **really tired of everyone always telling me how I got**
15   **treated badly by John and that I was the good one.**
16 JENNIE: **Excuse me? That's a bad thing?**
17 CORI: **Reaching a little, aren't you?**
18 SHELLY: **Not really. You just don't understand. See, John**
19   **wasn't so bad.** *(The girls react.)* **Honestly, he wasn't. But**
20   **you know what was bad? How everyone was always**
21   **telling him how wonderful I am and that he should be**
22   **happy to have me. It was like some sort of trigger that**
23   **made him want to explode. In fact, he told me when he**
24   **broke up with me that he wasn't good enough for me and**
25   **that I would be better off without him. So, here I am now,**
26   **without a boyfriend that I really liked because I am "too**
27   **good."**
28 NICOLE: **But he didn't deserve you.**
29 SHELLY: **In your opinion, Nicole. You don't know how he**
30   **was when we were alone. He was sweet and kind and**
31   **gentle. I really miss him. And he's gone because all of my**
32   **friends were "protecting" me.**
33 CORI: *(After a moment of uncomfortable silence as they all look*
34   *at the very quiet SHELLY)* **I'm really sorry, Shel.**
35 JENNIE: **Me, too.**

1   LORI: All of us are.

2   NICOLE: Not me.

3   CORI: Good bonding moment, Nicole.

4   NICOLE: Hey, I'm sorry, but I'm glad they broke up. OK, you

5   remember what I said about being honest? Well, here's

6   the rest of it. That little slime ball came on to me.

7   SHELLY: What?

8   NICOLE: Remember when I came over and you were in your

9   room getting dressed for Teri's party? And John was

10   waiting with me in the living room? Well, the worm

11   actually had the nerve to tell me that he wanted to see

12   me after the party was over and he dropped you off at

13   home. He said, "Meet me at The Diner and then we'll go

14   some place and talk." And he said talk in a way that made

15   it absolutely clear there was to be no talking involved.

16   LORI: Why didn't you tell us?

17   NICOLE: Because it wasn't anyone's business. But I told him

18   that I *would* tell Shelly if he didn't. And then I *did* tell

19   him that he didn't deserve you. So, if you're mad at me,

20   I'm sorry, but I'm very glad you broke up.

21   SHELLY: Oh . . . he actually did that?

22   NICOLE: Yep.

23   SHELLY: *(After a pause)* *That pig!* OK, positive stuff. I knew

24   he was messing around with other girls. But I never knew

25   that he came on to you. You know Jessica? She couldn't

26   wait to throw it in my face.

27   JENNIE: I hate that chick.

28   LORI: Tramp, pure and simple.

29   SHELLY: But finding out that he did that with you, and you

30   put your friendship with me first. Not many other girls

31   would do that.

32   CORI: Not many other people have the bonds we do.

33   NICOLE: Shelly, you know that you mean way more to me

34   than any stupid little high school jerky boy.

35   SHELLY: Yeah, I know, but it's nice to have it reinforced. I

1 can't *believe* that fool. Did any of you know about this?

2 *(They respond with no's.)*

3 NICOLE: Like I said, I didn't want to hurt you.

4 LORI: And I thought I could keep a secret!

5 SHELLY: Thank you, Nicole. See? What other girls on this

6 campus have this kind of loyalty? Oh! Add loyalty to the

7 list of love, acceptance and trust.

8 CORI: Now it's my turn. Incense stick please.

9 LORI: Hand it the other way, please. My sinuses are swelling

10 to three times their normal size.

11 JENNIE: Lori, shut up.

12 LORI: I know you say that out of love.

13 CORI: My negative comment is easy.

14 LORI: Great.

15 SHELLY: Oh, fine, Cori.

16 JENNIE: How nice.

17 NICOLE: The rest of us at least took a minute to think.

18 CORI: Well, I've been thinking about this for a long time. This

19 is why I came up with this idea, so we could get this kind

20 of stuff out in the open.

21 SHELLY: So, shoot.

22 CORI: OK. My negative comment is that whenever we all get

23 together no one ever wants to come over to my house.

24 *(The girls look at each other, uncomfortable with this truth.)* I

25 mean, I know why, but sometimes I feel that you think

26 that just because my family isn't the nicest or happiest

27 in the world, that it might rub off on you, like cooties or

28 something. I get tired, too, of hearing my mom and dad

29 scream at each other. Of my brothers fighting. But,

30 sometimes they all aren't home and we can go over there

31 and go to my room and I can share myself and who I am

32 with you. But we never do.

33 LORI: Cori, I'm really sorry. But, it's just so . . . I don't know.

34 CORI: I do. It's uncomfortable. But my room. It's like this

35 little insulated island in an ocean of unhappiness. I

1   painted it and re-did the curtains and bed and put up
2   these really zen-like posters. I really want to share that
3   with you. Because — and here's the positive stuff —
4   because you guys are the only real family I have. I can
5   come to you and feel accepted and not get yelled at. If I
6   need a hug, I can get one, because my dad and mom sure
7   aren't going to do it. I really need some people that I can
8   love and be loved by. And since God, for whatever reason,
9   chose not to give me relatives I can share that with, he
10 gave me you.
11 JENNIE: Oh, Cori. Dammit, now I am going to cry.
12 SHELLY: We'll always be here for you, won't we guys?
13 LORI: For you, Cori, and for each other.
14 NICOLE: Group hug, group hug. *(They do, and all quietly begin*
15 *singing.)*
16 ALL: Kumbah ya, my Lord, Kumbah ya.
17 CORI: See, we'll never, ever forget this, will we?
18
19
20
21
22
23
24
25
26
27
28
29
30
31
32
33
34
35

1 ## YOU KNOW WHAT I MEAN?
2
3 *(This monolog should be presented with very little breathing between*
4 *thoughts. She just begins and then GOES!)*
5
6 The weirdest thing happened. I was leaving Spanish class
7 minding my own business, just walking along to algebra. Don't
8 you hate algebra? I mean you have to learn all these dumb
9 formulas and tell me, when does x ever really stand for
10 anything anyone really needs? I mean, I know that I will never
11 really have to use x for anything real, ever. Anyway, I was
12 walking along talking to Debra. Does she annoy you as much
13 as me? I mean if I have to listen to her go on and on about
14 Darrell anymore I will just have to puke all over her brand
15 new snakeskin shoes. And who really needs snake on their
16 shoes? I mean, I'm sure the snake misses that skin more than
17 the shoes need it, don't you think? I make it a policy to never
18 wear anything or eat anything that has a face. You know what
19 I mean? It's just the way I feel. Anyway, here was Debra going
20 on and on, Darrell this and Darrell that. Darrell. What a stupid
21 name, huh? How old-fashioned and out of date, but that's kind
22 of like Darrell anyway. Can you believe he actually wanted
23 to vote Republican? Thank God he's not eighteen yet and we
24 didn't get his vote. Not that he probably would have voted
25 anyway. Voting is something I take very seriously. Not like
26 some people my age who just talk about it. I would actually
27 go and vote. I feel very strongly about this. But you know
28 some people just go on and on but never really say anything,
29 you know what I mean? Anyway, here I was, walking down
30 the hall with snakeskin shoe Deb and her Darrell monolog
31 when who should come out of Mr. Rosenberg's calculus class
32 but Tom. *Yes, Tom!* I could have died. I tried to turn around
33 and walk the other way, but here comes Mr. Rosenberg yelling,
34 "Hey, Sarah, missed you in class today." Now, I know I wasn't
35 in class, and he knows I wasn't in class, and now everybody

1   knows I wasn't in class. Like it's everybody's business, right?
2   I mean, did he have to yell out like that? So, I had to stop and
3   try to explain to him why I wasn't in class, not that he would
4   listen because he never does listen to anyone else. Don't you
5   hate people that go on and on like that? I mean, they never
6   say what they mean, they just go on and on in like this stream
7   of consciousness thing that gets really annoying. So it's like
8   they start out to say something and then totally go off in a
9   whole different direction and it gets to be really stupid, you
10 know what I mean? So I told Mr. Rosenberg that I had "my
11 time" this morning. That shut him up good. Men, they never
12 know what to say when you give them that answer. What do
13 men do when they need an excuse? They just don't have one,
14 you know? So maybe that's why they make up so many lies.
15 They don't have just the one that is irrefutable to help them
16 out. Anyway, I stood there talking to Mr. Rosenberg, trying
17 like a fiend to motion to Deb that Tom was coming but she
18 just kept right on walking, completely missing the fact that I
19 was no longer by her side. Talk about self-absorbed, right?
20 So, Mr. Rosenberg hears about the "my time" stuff, blushes
21 bright red and walks away. But then Tom heard it too. Or at
22 least I think he did because he just looked at me and then
23 turned around in a couple of circles like he didn't know where
24 he was going. But isn't that always the way with most men,
25 turning in circles, completely in a fog without a sensible
26 woman to guide them? My father is like that. He just goes
27 around and around in circles if my mother doesn't help him
28 get from one thought to the next. I mean, the man would starve
29 to death in front of a full refrigerator. But sometimes my mom
30 goes on and on and doesn't let dad get a word in edgewise.
31 Isn't that really annoying? She just talks and talks and talks
32 and makes no sense sometimes, you know what I mean?
33 Anyway . . . what was I saying?
34
35

1	**LINDA**
2	
3	*(LINDA is finally confronting her friend SHARON with her pent-up*
4	*feelings of frustration with their relationship.)*
5	
6	I don't get it. You've got everything going for you. You're
7	smart, you've got flair, style, talent, everything. What's the
8	deal? Why are you always in such a state of agony? God, just
9	give me half of what you've got, I'd be satisfied. I mean, just
10	once I'd like to look in a mirror and see you looking out at
11	me. I know you're scared to make a choice, but Sharon, we're
12	all afraid. You act like you're the only one who has anything
13	to lose here, but for God's sake, grow up! You are not the sun
14	and I am not the Mother Earth there to revolve around the
15	gravity of your feelings. It's time for me to break away from
16	all that excess emotional baggage you fling at me. I can't
17	absorb any more. So, Sharon, I will be your best friend, but I
18	can't be your emotional porter.
19	
20	
21	
22	
23	
24	
25	
26	
27	
28	
29	
30	
31	
32	
33	
34	
35	

AMY

(AMY discusses the indignity she has just suffered.)

You know, I just don't understand men today. Let me
rephrase that. I don't understand boys. See, I'm on *The Pill*,
but for strictly medical reasons, which I don't want to go into
at this moment in time. But when I told Billy, you should have
seen the look on his face. Like it was Christmas morning. He
seemed to think that because, as he so quaintly put it, things
were *taken care of*, that it was open season. But I said "No."
Then he started sweet-talking me, telling me how much he
loved me and that this would be the next logical step in our
relationship. And again, I said "No." So then he got a little
pouty and muttered that familiar line, "If you really loved me,
you would." Uh-huh. Right. I told him "No!" Then I added that
if he really loved me, he wouldn't keep asking. Then he had
the nerve to say that there were plenty of other girls out there
who would. That's when I walked to the door, opened it for
him, and told him good luck in his hunt to find one. He just
doesn't seem to understand that even though I can, I won't.
I'm just not ready to make that step. And guess what? I'm
proud that I stood my ground. I'm too precious to waste. He
doesn't deserve me. Out there somewhere is someone who is
waiting for me. I want to make sure that not only does that
special someone deserve me, but that I deserve him.

◆ BOYS ◆

THE ROAD YOU CHOOSE

FRANK: Has recently joined a gang. He has just been kicked off the football team.

RICK: Frank's former best friend, a good student and athlete.

SETTING: RICK enters the locker room and sees FRANK who is putting his things in his bag. RICK shakes his head in disgust. FRANK looks up, sees him, looks down, waits a moment and begins to speak.

FRANK: You got a problem, boy?

RICK: *(About to snap back, and while not afraid at all, thinks better of it.)* No, Frank, no problem.

FRANK: Then, what are you looking at, boy?

RICK: *(A long look, then)* I don't know, Frank. I really don't know.

FRANK: Listen, boy, you better watch that mouth of yours.

RICK: Ya think?

FRANK: Yeah, I do. I might just have to pound that pretty little face in.

RICK: Well, Frank, you know . . . I'm real scared. I think I just might die of fright. You are just such a big man.

FRANK: Listen, boy, you better be scared. You saw what I did to Eric.

RICK: No, Frank, I saw what you and your loser friends did to Eric. You were just a part of that gang that beat the hell out of him.

FRANK: Well, I think he got our message pretty effectively.

RICK: What message is that?

FRANK: Don't mess with the posse.

RICK: *(Mocking)* Don't mess with the *posse?* With the *posse?* Do you know how stupid you sound?

FRANK: You're pushing it, boy.

RICK: And don't call me boy, Frank.

FRANK: What are you going to do if I do, *boy?*

1　**RICK:** *(Getting in his face, low menacing voice)* **I can take care of**
2　　　**it, trust me.**
3　**FRANK:** *(Right back in his face, just as menacing)* **You want to**
4　　　**take me on right here? Right now?**
5　**RICK:** *(Looking at him, stepping back, not backing down)* **Yeah, I**
6　　　**would. But would you, without your loser friends around**
7　　　**to help you out?**
8　**FRANK:** **That's it, Rick. Come on, right now.**
9　**RICK:** **Well, at least you remember my name.**
10　**FRANK:** **I'll recognize it on your tombstone.** *(He goes after*
11　　　*RICK, who sidesteps him.)* **What's the matter, are you afraid?**
12　　　**You backing down?**
13　**RICK:** **You're not worth it, Frank.**
14　**FRANK:** **You're just afraid. Afraid to fight with a man, aren't**
15　　　**you, boy?**
16　**RICK:** **Look at you, Frank. What the hell is happening here?**
17　　　**You get kicked off the team, you're failing your classes,**
18　　　**you hang out with all these losers . . .**
19　**FRANK:** **Those losers are my friends.**
20　**RICK:** **My point, exactly.**
21　**FRANK:** **That's not what I meant. They aren't losers.**
22　**RICK:** **Yeah? What do you guys do? Hang out at the mall,**
23　　　**shoplift, pick up on chicks, go home. Oh, yeah. You might**
24　　　**gang up on someone now and then and beat the hell out**
25　　　**of him just for the exercise.**
26　**FRANK:** **You might be next, Rick, if you don't shut your**
27　　　**mouth.**
28　**RICK:** **What are you going to do now that you're off the team?**
29　**FRANK:** **Hey, it's just as well. Practice is for losers.**
30　**RICK:** **Oh, OK. I get it. Just the cool people get kicked off the**
31　　　**team so they can do more mall hanging.**
32　**FRANK:** *(Picking up his bag and heading for the door)* **Take this as**
33　　　**a warning. Watch your back. We'll be there.**
34　**RICK:** *(To FRANK's back)* **Lisa said hi.**
35　**FRANK:** *(Stopping, not turning)* **She did?**

1   RICK: Yeah.
2   FRANK: *(Turning around)* **What else did she say?**
3   RICK: Nothing.
4   FRANK: When did you see her?
5   RICK: When I picked up Eric after you and your gang got
6   through with him.
7   FRANK: Did you say anything?
8   RICK: No. It was none of my business, but now I guess I'll
9   make it my business.
10 FRANK: What? Why?
11 RICK: Because she's my cousin and I don't think it's a good
12   idea if you see her anymore.
13 FRANK: I haven't seen her since last summer at the river.
14 RICK: You've called her, haven't you?
15 FRANK: Once in a while. Does she talk about me?
16 RICK: Yeah.
17 FRANK: What's she say?
18 RICK: How nice you are and how much fun last summer was
19   at the river.
20 FRANK: Oh. Yeah ...
21 RICK: *(Looking evenly at him, almost waiting for a response)* **Uh-huh.**
22 FRANK: Tell her hi, OK?
23 RICK: Nah, I don't think so.
24 FRANK: Why not?
25 RICK: Because the Frank she knew is long gone. The Frank
26   that came every summer to the river with my family,
27   dated my favorite cousin, learned to jet ski and water
28   ski with my father — that Frank died the minute he
29   joined a gang.
30 FRANK: Hey, man, it's about survival.
31 RICK: No, man, it's about choices. You made the choice, you
32   didn't have to take that road.
33 FRANK: You don't know what you're talking about. You
34   don't know what it's like. You don't need to feel the
35   support, because you've grown up with all the things I

1   never had.

2   RICK: Bull! We grew up together. My mom got to where she

3   just automatically set a place for you at dinner. We spent

4   the night at each other's house all the time. We've gone

5   to the same schools, had the same teachers, same

6   friends ... until now. My mom asks me all the time,

7   "Where's Frank?" I just tell her that you're busy.

8   FRANK: I am.

9   RICK: Doing what? What the hell do you do all day? God

10   knows you're not in class.

11   FRANK: I hang out with my friends.

12   RICK: Very cool.

13   FRANK: You know, because of our history, I am trying very

14   hard not to beat the crap out of you.

15   RICK: Don't do me any favors, Frank. If I recall correctly,

16   anytime we fought, I always won.

17   FRANK: That was before.

18   RICK: Oh, right. Before when it was just one on one. Now, I

19   guess it will be one on, oh, what? Six or eight?

20   FRANK: Just take my warning, OK?

21   RICK: You'd actually do it, wouldn't you? You'd really have

22   your loser friends come after me.

23   FRANK: Yeah, I would. Things change, Rick. Learn to change

24   with them. Keep in mind who has the power.

25   RICK: Yeah, I'll remember that when I'm at college and

26   you're hanging on the corner with your friends waiting

27   for your big job at Burger King to open up.

28   FRANK: I don't need college to be a success.

29   RICK: No? What are you going to do? *(Facetiously)* Sell drugs?

30   *(FRANK doesn't answer.)* **Jeez.**

31   FRANK: You tell me some other way to make good money

32   without a college degree.

33   RICK: Then go to college.

34   FRANK: How? You have no problem, mister athletic scholar-

35   ship jock.

1   RICK: I worked hard for that scholarship, Frank. Both on the
2   field and in the classroom.
3   FRANK: Always looking for the way to kiss the butt of the
4   next teacher, aren't you?
5   RICK: You look at it anyway you want to. I just know that we
6   started off in the same place and are ending up in
7   completely different worlds.
8   FRANK: You had way more opportunities than I ever did.
9   RICK: Face it, Frank. You made your own choices when you
10   decided to become one of the defeated masses. It's your
11   choice to not go to classes, your choice to hang out with
12   guys whose idea of success is how much they can score
13   on the next deal. You had the same opportunities I did.
14   You just made different choices. Live with it. *(They look*
15   *at each other, saying nothing.)*
16   FRANK: *(After a moment)* See you around, Rick.
17   RICK: I doubt it. *(FRANK gives him a look of surprise at this*
18   *remark when he has just made an overture.)* Frank, we don't
19   know each other anymore. I really doubt that we'll be
20   seeing each other around.
21   FRANK: Yeah. I guess not. *(As he exits)* Remember me to Lisa.
22   RICK: *(Calling after him)* I will. *(FRANK is gone. Quietly, to*
23   *himself)* No, I don't think so.
24
25
26
27
28
29
30
31
32
33
34
35

A NEW ATTITUDE

CHAD: Eighteen, has found that being rude gets him girls.

JOHN: Eighteen, his honest and sensitive friend.

SETTING: CHAD and JOHN, sitting on the school steps, discuss their feelings about a new school year and a new attitude with which to face it.

CHAD: **Another school year begins, but this year we are seniors. The world is our oyster.**

JOHN: **I just hope I graduate.**

CHAD: **Graduate? The least of my worries. I have more than enough units. I, my friend, my pal, my buddy, plan on concentrating on the babes.**

JOHN: **The babes? And is that how you intend to refer to the girls this year?**

CHAD: **That or some other form of endearment. The honeys. The chicks. The wenches. The bettys.**

JOHN: **And I am assuming you plan on spending your time alone, without female comfort?**

CHAD: *(Seeing a girl walk by)* **Hey, baby, bring it over here.** *(She responds, and although we cannot hear it, we pretty much get the idea.)* **Stuck up bitch.**

JOHN: **That's treating the woman with respect, Chad. Good job. I'm sure you will have the women falling at your feet.**

CHAD: **Hey, I'm a senior and this is my year to howl. I've worked hard for the last three years so I could take it easy, this my final year of being a kid. I plan on partying, on getting together with as many dolls as I can.**

JOHN: **What's with you? Why are you talking like such an idiot?**

CHAD: **Idiot? Hardly. Think about it, John. Who, over the last three years, have we seen get most of the women? Has it been us? No, it has not. It has been guys like Matt, like Josh, like Charles. And have they treated the girls at this**

1   school like women who deserve respect? I ask you.

2   JOHN: So Matt, Josh and Charles are your new role models?

3   Just because they treat women like dirt doesn't mean it's

4   the thing to do.

5   CHAD: Of course it's not the thing to do. It's not nice. It's not

6   polite, it's not kind. But it sure works for them, doesn't

7   it? When was the last time you saw any of those guys at

8   a party alone?

9   JOHN: *(Thinking)* I don't remember.

10   CHAD: That's because there is nothing to remember. They

11   always have girls climbing all over them. And why?

12   Because they act like they don't care. And what about us?

13   JOHN: I care. I treat the girls with dignity and respect.

14   CHAD: And they love you, right?

15   JOHN: I have a lot of girls who like me.

16   CHAD: As a friend, John, as a friend. How many more times

17   do you need to hear, "You're like a brother to me"? Look

18   at Charles. Has any girl ever said that to him? No, they

19   haven't.

20   JOHN: But you should hear how the girls talk about him. The

21   names they call him, how he makes them cry.

22   CHAD: And how do you know all this?

23   JOHN: Well, Jenny called me when she found out Charles

24   was cheating on her with Tammy. And then when Patty

25   found Matt with that new girl Janice, she called me.

26   CHAD: Uh-huh. Go on.

27   JOHN: OK, there was the time Adam promised to take both

28   Kimi and Laura to the prom and then ended up going

29   with Chandra. I spent that whole prom night with Kimi

30   and Laura trying to console them.

31   CHAD: I think my point is being made.

32   JOHN: What do you mean?

33   CHAD: John, aren't you tired of being every girl's best friend?

34   Isn't it getting a little old treating girls with respect and

35   then having them pat you on your head, say thanks and

1		watch them go out with one of the guys they just spent
2		hours crying over?
3	JOHN:	Oh. I think I see where you're going with this.
4	CHAD:	I spent the whole summer thinking about this.
5	JOHN:	And what did you come up with?
6	CHAD:	Well, while my family and I spent the summer at the
7		river, there was a bunch of new people there. Girls I had
8		never met before, who didn't know me.
9	JOHN:	Well, they didn't know you. You were ahead just on
10		that point alone.
11	CHAD:	Do you want to hear this, or not?
12	JOHN:	Sorry. Go on.
13	CHAD:	Thank you. So, anyway, I tried out this new attitude
14		on them. And guess what?
15	JOHN:	What?
16	CHAD:	I had a date every night. They were calling me,
17		coming over, bringing me homemade cookies. And this
18		was all the time. It was weird.
19	JOHN:	What'd you do that was different?
20	CHAD:	I was rude, but in a funny way. I found out they liked
21		funny, as long as they were not the butt of the joke. They
22		especially liked it when I talked about some other girl.
23		That's a big one. Also, if I never said I'd call them, they
24		made a point to ask me to call. Or else they called me!
25		And never, ever make a commitment to any of them. Date
26		them all. It seems like the more girls I dated, the more
27		girls wanted to date me.
28	JOHN:	So, you mean if you treated them like you didn't care
29		about any of them, they wanted you?
30	CHAD:	Exactly!
31	JOHN:	It seems stupid and phony to me.
32	CHAD:	To me, too. But, damn it, it works for everyone else.
33		And I, for one, do not plan on spending my senior year
34		being a soggy shoulder for the tears of some stupid girl
35		as she cries over some other guy.

1   JOHN: How did it make you feel, treating them like that?
2   CHAD: It's funny. At first I felt really bad. But after a while,
3   .   I kinda got used to it. As a matter of fact, I liked it a lot.
4   JOHN: You like being a jerk to women?
5   CHAD: Well, when you put it that way, no. But when I see
6   that this is what seems to work, what the hell, huh? *(Seeing*
7   *another girl)* Hey, baby.
8   JOHN: Hey, baby?! I can't say that. That's just rude. You don't
9   call girls names like that.
10   CHAD: I didn't call her a name. *(He looks in the girl's direction*
11   *and winks, turns back to JOHN with a big smile.)* Did you see
12   that? She waved, she smiled, she loved it.
13   JOHN: I can't do it.
14   CHAD: It's easy. And did you see her? She looked at me like I
15   was someone.
16   JOHN: Until she recognized it was you. Did you see her look
17   at you like you had lost your mind?
18   CHAD: Well, I don't expect this new system to work right
19   away. I've got to hone it, perfect it.
20   JOHN: Face it, Chad. You're never going to be able to carry
21   this off at this school. Everyone knows you.
22   CHAD: What? A person can't change?
23   JOHN: Not that much.
24   CHAD: Well, I'm going to try. I saw Amber this morning. I
25   told her I'd call her tonight.
26   JOHN: Well, that's good. She's nice. She's a good person.
27   CHAD: Exactly! So, I'm not going to call.
28   JOHN: You're not going to call? Why?
29   CHAD: Haven't you been listening? Because she expects me
30   to. In the past, when I said I was going to call a girl, I
31   would. Well, this time, I'm not. You watch. Tomorrow,
32   first thing in the morning, she will come up and give me
33   a hard time for not calling. I will apologize. *(He pretends*
34   *JOHN is Amber, puts his arm around him.)* Babe, sorry. I
35   totally forgot. I was really busy. But, honestly kitty cat,

1   I'll call tonight. Forgive me?

2 JOHN: Kitty cat?

3 CHAD: Yeah. Good, huh? I've got a whole list of names I

4   came up with to call girls. And you watch. It will work.

5   It's worked for those other guys for years.

6 JOHN: That doesn't mean it's right.

7 CHAD: I know it doesn't. But just because it's not right

8   doesn't mean it doesn't work. See?

9 JOHN: And this is how you spent your summer? Coming up

10   with ways to get women?

11 CHAD: What better way to spend your days off?

12 JOHN: Well, you do what you want. I can't act like that.

13 CHAD: Do what you want. But trust me. When we are at the

14   next party, and you go in a corner with some girl it won't

15   be to neck, it will be to hear the story of how I am such

16   a jerk and why does she like me so much.

17 JOHN: And you'll be proud of this?

18 CHAD: Proud. Proud isn't what I want. I want action. I want

19   play. I've had proud. It doesn't work with these girls.

20 JOHN: It works with girls who are worth it.

21 CHAD: Well, you just point one out to me that hasn't been

22   with one of the jerks and then we'll talk.

23 JOHN: I can't believe you are really going to try this.

24 CHAD: Oh, no? Well, look over there at that bevy of bettys.

25   I'm going to try it out now. Watch my smoke. *(He exits.)*

26   Hey, wenches, how ya doin'?

27 JOHN: Bevy of bettys? What the hell is that? *(He shakes his*

28   *head and exits in opposite direction.)*

29

30

31

32

33

34

35

DIVORCE, AMERICAN STYLE

JEFF: Seventeen. His parents are divorcing and he's moving away.

PAUL: Also 17. Confused and angry about his friend's situation.

SETTING: PAUL enters JEFF's room, watching him pack his carry-on bag for the upcoming trip.

JEFF: *(Noticing PAUL at the door)* **Hey, Paul ... how you doing?**

PAUL: *(Quietly)* **I'm OK. So, you almost packed?**

JEFF: **Yeah.** *(Indicating small bag)* **Got all my carry-on stuff here. Toothbrush, deodorant, sandwich in case the plane crashes and I have to survive on my own.**

PAUL: *(A weak smile)* **Great. Well, you've always been prepared for everything. Wish I could say the same.**

JEFF: **Yeah ... well.** *(After a moment)* **This is really weird.**

PAUL: **I know. Hey, you be sure to write to me, OK?**

JEFF: **Like you have to even ask.**

PAUL: **Well, I know what it's like. You'll get busy, I'll get busy. Pretty soon, we're so busy we don't have time for old friends.**

JEFF: **It will never be that way with us. Amigos forever.** *(He holds out his hand.)*

PAUL: *(Shaking his hand)* **Forever.** *(They hug impulsively.)* **God, I feel like a stupid girl. This is ridiculous.**

JEFF: **I know. I thought only women acted like this when their best friends moved.**

PAUL: **I can't believe that in January, when school starts again, you'll be gone.**

JEFF: **Yeah, who are you gonna mooch a ride from?**

PAUL: **No kidding. No, really, what am I gonna do? Who am I gonna hang out with?**

JEFF: **There's plenty of people. Mark, Jay, Brad, all of them.**

PAUL: **I know, but Jeff ... they aren't like, you know, my best friend ... I swear I feel like some freshman girl whining about her friend leaving.**

1   JEFF: Emotion is not the sole territory of women.
2   PAUL: Well, public displays of it are, or should be. *(Deep*
3   *breath to maintain control)* **Dammit.**
4   JEFF: Paul, it's not like I'm moving to another country.
5   PAUL: No, just across state lines. Five of them.
6   JEFF: Well, how do you think I feel? My whole life is being
7   turned upside down. I'm leaving my friends, my home,
8   and whatever family I once had is gone.
9   PAUL: Your parents are sure they want this divorce?
10 JEFF: Oh, yeah. Trust me. They want it in a big way. In fact,
11   this is the first time in years that they have actually sat
12   down and had a discussion that didn't degenerate into
13   objects being tossed at one another.
14 PAUL: When is your dad getting married?
15 JEFF: As soon as the final papers are signed.
16 PAUL: What are you going to call your new stepmother?
17 JEFF: Well, so far I've been getting by on "Uh, excuse me . . ."
18   I think pretty soon my dad is going to expect me to start
19   using some noun or another.
20 PAUL: What about "Mom"?
21 JEFF: I'm sorry, but I just can't see myself calling some
22   twenty-five-year-old blonde chick named Tiffany "Mom."
23   Not in this lifetime.
24 PAUL: How about "Babe"?
25 JEFF: Oh, yeah, that would go over real well.
26 PAUL: I bet. *(There is an awkward pause.)* So, the house sold,
27   huh?
28 JEFF: Yep. Quick, too. It seems like they put it up for sale one
29   day and the next day, it was gone . . . just gone.
30 PAUL: No arguing over division of property?
31 JEFF: *(Ironic laugh)* Only one thing, the dog. Neither of them
32   wants good old Slug.
33 PAUL: An aptly named dog.
34 JEFF: Hey, hey, watch what you say about Slug. He may be a
35   disgusting, smelly, hair-losing, ear-missing, flea-infested

1   **bag of bones, but he's been this man's best friend for ten**
2   **years.**
3   PAUL: So, who gets him?
4   JEFF: I told my parents, whoever takes me, takes Slug. Love
5   me, love my dog.
6   PAUL: So, he's going with you and your mom?
7   JEFF: It was a toss-up there for a while, but yeah. It looked
8   for a time like they were gonna fight over who had to
9   take me, too.
10   PAUL: I can't believe it.
11   JEFF: Tell me about it.
12   PAUL: They are so stinking selfish.
13   JEFF: I know.
14   PAUL: You'd think that they'd care a little more about you
15   and a little less about themselves.
16   JEFF: Yeah . . .
17   PAUL: It gets me so mad, every time I think about how stupid
18   your parents are acting.
19   JEFF: Well, you know . . .
20   PAUL: Divorce, moving, *bam!* "Pack it up, Jeff, we're outta
21   here."
22   JEFF: Well, it wasn't exactly . . .
23   PAUL: Did they even ask your opinion?
24   JEFF: To be honest . . .
25   PAUL: I didn't think so. Your parents have always been like
26   that.
27   JEFF: Like that . . . like what?
28   PAUL: Thinking only of what their needs are, not giving a
29   damn about you and what's going on in your life.
30   JEFF: Now, wait a min . . .
31   PAUL: *(Picking up steam)* And you always stick up for them.
32   *(Quoting JEFF)* "Oh, my dad cares about my game, he just
33   has to work or he'd be here." He never made it, though,
34   did he?
35   JEFF: Well, he did . . .

1   PAUL: *(Again quoting JEFF)* "Oh, my mom can't come hear
2   me sing tonight because she has a meeting."
3   JEFF: Sometimes, she can't make it . . .
4   PAUL: Did they ever ask your opinion about this?
5   JEFF: Well . . .
6   PAUL: I didn't think so. Just all the time, them and never a
7   thought for you.
8   JEFF: Wait a minute now. You act like my parents were
9   abusive or something.
10   PAUL: Hard to abuse someone you never pay attention to.
11   JEFF: Hey, they paid attention.
12   PAUL: Oh, yeah, like when it was time to go shopping for
13   school clothes or something, your mom was more than
14   happy to be with you . . . probably so she could pick
15   herself up a few things and in the meantime, buy your
16   love.
17   JEFF: It wasn't like that. We had some great times together.
18   PAUL: As a family? When? Name the time.
19   JEFF: Holidays . . .
20   PAUL: Face it, Jeffster, your holidays were spent with me
21   and my parents.
22   JEFF: On Christmas mornings we always opened presents
23   together as a family.
24   PAUL: Is that why you have been at my house by 8:00 a.m.
25   every Christmas morning since the second grade?
26   JEFF: We . . . well . . . we get up early and then . . .
27   PAUL: Then you come over to my house.
28   JEFF: What about the Fourth of July? Our whole family was
29   together.
30   PAUL: Yeah, at my house, my pool, my dad barbecuing and
31   you and I doing the fireworks. *(He looks at JEFF who has
32   no response.)*
33   JEFF: *(After a moment)* Damn. What the hell am I going to do?
34   PAUL: What do you mean?
35   JEFF: You're right. My closest and most loving relative is a

1		dog named Slug.

1   dog named Slug.

2   PAUL: So, what are you going to do about it?

3   JEFF: Do ... ?

4   PAUL: *(Excited)* I've been talking it over with my parents.

5   They said you could stay with us.

6   JEFF: They did?

7   PAUL: Listen, Jeff, it's not like it would be anything that

8   much different. You practically live at our house anyway.

9   JEFF: My parents probably wouldn't even notice that I

10   wasn't with either one of them.

11   PAUL: Right. So, do you want to?

12   JEFF: I'd have to ask.

13   PAUL: Why? You've been taking care of yourself for years.

14   JEFF: That's right! I'm a man ... practically.

15   PAUL: It would be great. Since Ted's away at college you can

16   have his room.

17   JEFF: He won't mind?

18   PAUL: Why should he? He's not there to use it. Besides, you're

19   practically like a brother to him, too.

20   JEFF: But my parents. I need to talk to them.

21   PAUL: So, go talk.

22   JEFF: *(Starting to leave)* OK, I will ... *(He stops.)*

23   PAUL: Well? Let's go.

24   JEFF: Paul, I can't.

25   PAUL: Why not? What's the problem?

26   JEFF: They're my parents.

27   PAUL: Has anyone told them?

28   JEFF: That's enough. You've spent the last ten minutes doing

29   nothing but badmouthing my mom and dad. They may

30   not be perfect ...

31   PAUL: You can say that again ...

32   JEFF: I said that was enough! Maybe we're not the typical

33   American family, but I love them. I can't just tell them

34   I'm leaving them.

35   PAUL: They didn't have any problem telling you, did they?

1   JEFF: It's not the same.

2   PAUL: It's exactly the same. You're trying to save a family

3   that doesn't exist anymore. Your father's moving to New

4   York to marry some dumb little blonde named Tiffany,

5   and your mom is dragging you to New Mexico so she can

6   open the new corporate office. By the time either of them

7   noticed you weren't there Dad would have already

8   started the second family and Mom will be figuring out

9   her next move up the corporate ladder.

10 JEFF: They love me.

11 PAUL: I know they do. In their own way. And I bet they'd

12   love you enough to let you go.

13 JEFF: *(Thinking a moment)* I don't know anyone in New Mexico.

14 PAUL: That's right.

15 JEFF: And I'm sure that Tiffany would be thrilled to have

16   Dad all to herself.

17 PAUL: True.

18 JEFF: The worst that could happen is they say no, right?

19 PAUL: Yeah.

20 JEFF: What the hell. I'll just tell them. I won't even ask. I

21   mean, if I present it to them as a done deal, maybe they'll

22   see that I can make adult decisions and they don't have

23   to worry about me.

24 PAUL: I think you're right.

25 JEFF: OK, I'm doing it. I'll go talk to my mom now.

26 PAUL: What about your dad?

27 JEFF: He's over at Tiffany's. She has him picking out colors

28   for the new apartment. She likes pink.

29 PAUL: *(Sarcastic)* I'm shocked.

30 JEFF: OK. I'm going.

31 PAUL: Great. I'll wait here. *(JEFF starts out.)* Hey, can I use

32   your phone?

33 JEFF: Yeah, go ahead. I don't know how long this will take.

34   She might put up a big fight.

35 PAUL: I'll be here.

1   **JEFF:**   **Wish me luck.** *(He leaves.)*

2   **PAUL:**   *(Dialing the phone, he speaks into it.)* **Mom? It's me. Yeah,**

3   **I talked to him ... No, I made him think it was his**

4   **idea ... No, he doesn't have any idea that his mom**

5   **already talked to you ... Are you kidding? How do you**

6   **think I'd feel if I found out neither of my parents wanted**

7   **me ... Yeah, we'll be home in time for dinner ...** *(About*

8   *to hang up, he calls into the phone.)* **Hey, Mom, I love you.**

9

10

11

12

13

14

15

16

17

18

19

20

21

22

23

24

25

26

27

28

29

30

31

32

33

34

35

IT'S ONLY A GAME

JEFF: Football player with no team spirit.

KEVIN: A dedicated team player, Jeff's friend.

TOM: Another friend, also a team player.

SETTING: KEVIN, JEFF and TOM are discussing the team's efforts of the night before.

KEVIN: You know, I am getting really tired of losing. Really tired.

JEFF: It wouldn't be so bad if we just lost — but the massacres we've had to take. Tom, what was the final score last night?

TOM: You were there. You saw the scoreboard, didn't you?

JEFF: After a while I just didn't look anymore.

KEVIN: Even when the coach made us stare at the scoreboard for the full sixty seconds after the game?

JEFF: Was that the dumbest thing he's ever made us do, or what? I just refused to look.

TOM: Well, I looked. I stared. The full sixty seconds looking at "Home Team: twenty-eight; Visiting Team: zero." You never realize how slow sixty seconds can go until it's used to humiliate you.

KEVIN: The worst was sitting there in the end zone, in front of the opposing team and the crowd and just looking in silence.

JEFF: That's why I didn't do it. I don't need this kind of humiliation. I get enough of that at my own school without having it done to me on foreign soil.

KEVIN: Well, the coach had a point to make, I think.

JEFF: A point? And what would that be, Kevin? It sure couldn't be anything positive. I know that I felt bad enough without having my face rubbed in it in front of everyone.

TOM: Jeff, the coach wanted us to look at the board as a team

1 and feel that we should band together as a team to do
2 better next time.
3 JEFF: Oh, yeah. I know I'm inspired to go out there and do
4 my best now. Degradation is a real positive method of
5 reinforcing team values.
6 KEVIN: You know what your problem is? Your problem is
7 that you are not a team player.
8 JEFF: Hey, no one out there works harder than me at
9 practice.
10 TOM: Well, you might work hard, but you don't join in.
11 KEVIN: Tom's right. You are out there physically but you
12 are not with us mentally. Football is a mental game.
13 JEFF: You're telling me that Matt, Adam, Dominic, Brian,
14 and the rest of those remedial readers are mentally more
15 aware than I am?
16 TOM: That's not the point, Jeff. What it is, is the fact that you
17 just don't become a part of a team, a unit.
18 KEVIN: You alienate yourself from the team. Not joining in
19 last night when the coach told us to look at the score is
20 a good example.
21 JEFF: You guys are going to stand there and tell me that you
22 looked at the score the whole time he told you to?
23 KEVIN: Yes. I felt that if the coach told us to do it, he had a
24 good reason.
25 TOM: And it was something we were told to do as a team.
26 JEFF: So, if the coach told the team to run naked in the
27 streets, you would do that?
28 TOM: Don't be an idiot.
29 KEVIN: But, if the coach told us to do that, he'd have a reason,
30 don't you think?
31 JEFF: Kevin, are you completely stupid? Or is it just a short
32 brain spasm from too many hits last night?
33 KEVIN: You know, that is your problem. Every time the
34 coaches tell us to do something, you have one of your
35 snappy little comebacks to make. You can't just go along

1   with the rest of the team, can you?

2 JEFF: I guess I'm just not a follower like the rest of the

3   lemmings. That's what happens when you use your own

4   mind.

5 TOM: No, what happens is that the team falls apart, which is

6   what is going on now. This team has never had this kind

7   of trouble before.

8 JEFF: What do you mean, "this team"?

9 KEVIN: He's right. Our school has always been successful.

10   It's just this year we seem to have lost it.

11 JEFF: Maybe the coaches aren't doing their job right. Maybe

12   they need us to talk to them.

13 KEVIN: Oh, please, Jeff, can I be there when you do that? I'm

14   sure Coach Molna would be happy to have your input.

15 TOM: I'd like to see that.

16 JEFF: I'm serious. Obviously something is not going right.

17   Maybe we should form a committee to talk to the coaches,

18   give them some ideas. You know, not all of us are the

19   mental deficients they treat us like.

20 KEVIN: They don't treat us like mental deficients. They

21   treat us like a team.

22 JEFF: But we are individuals first, aren't we? Don't you think

23   that should be addressed?

24 TOM: No, as a matter of fact, I don't. We need to be treated as

25   a team, a singular working unit.

26 JEFF: I don't know about you, Tom, but I am an individual

27   first. I am tired of being called "guys" or "team" or

28   "starters" or worse yet, "ladies."

29 KEVIN: Oh, so you want the coaches to name each of us one

30   at a time?

31 JEFF: I think I would like, just once in a while, to be talked to

32   like a human being.

33 TOM: The point is, though, that we are not human beings out

34   there on the field. We are, or at least should be, one

35   working unit that has one major goal which is to win.

1   JEFF: But if the individual has no singular pride, then why
2   should the individual work with a team?
3   KEVIN: You guys, we're talking football here, not philosophy.
4   It's a game. Just a game.
5   JEFF: Exactly. It's a game. And if it is just a game, why is
6   everyone's ego so wrapped up in our winning. Shouldn't
7   we just go out there, have a good time, win or lose, and
8   go home?
9   TOM: You're missing the point, Jeff.
10 JEFF: You know, that's like the third time you have said
11   something to me about not getting the point. Is that a
12   reference to the ball I dropped?
13 TOM: No. But now that you mention it, I guess it could be.
14 JEFF: It's not my fault I dropped the ball. Doug just can't
15   throw worth crap.
16 KEVIN: Doug can throw fine. You're just so busy out there
17   hot dogging it that you don't pay attention. You're always
18   one step behind the rest of us.
19 JEFF: So, are you saying it's my fault we lost the game?
20 KEVIN: You were a big part of it. Did you catch a single pass
21   that was sent to you?
22 JEFF: Did you?
23 KEVIN: Not all of them, but at least I admit that I didn't do as
24   good a job as I could have. But you won't admit it about
25   yourself.
26 JEFF: All right, fine. I didn't do as well as I could have. But I
27   get so tired of the guys on this team and their attitudes.
28   It's so stupid to do that huddle yell. And that warm-up
29   routine is embarrassing.
30 TOM: We do that stuff to build up team spirit.
31 JEFF: All it does is make us look like idiots.
32 TOM: You are really a piece of work, you know that, Jeff?
33   You really are. You are the first to put down someone
34   when they screw up, but it's never your fault. You are
35   the first to walk to the locker room, get changed and get

1   out. You never hang out with the rest of the team, talk
2   over the game, hang around.
3   JEFF: I've got other things to do than hang out with a bunch
4   of dumb jocks.
5   KEVIN: Then, maybe you shouldn't be on this team.
6   JEFF: Just because I don't want to hang out?
7   KEVIN: Part of being on a team is actually *being* on the team.
8   You make an effort to separate yourself.
9   JEFF: I hang out with you guys.
10 TOM: That's only because you'd hang out with us anyway.
11   Kevin and I also make it a point to get together with the
12   other guys on the team.
13 JEFF: I don't have time for it.
14 TOM: No, you don't make time. Remember hell week?
15   Every day the whole team was invited over to Laurie's
16   house so the cheerleaders could feed us. Did you go?
17 JEFF: I went once.
18 KEVIN: One time. Big deal. The rest of the team went every day.
19 TOM: We ate, we talked, the coaches were there. It was like a
20   family.
21 JEFF: I've got a family. I don't need a surrogate one.
22 TOM: No one is saying you do. But the fact remains that we
23   bonded as a team and you just aren't a part of that.
24 JEFF: So what you're saying is that we are playing lousy
25   football because I didn't go eat some stale meal with a
26   bunch of stupid cheerleaders and sweaty players.
27 KEVIN: Forget it, Tom. He just doesn't see what we mean.
28 JEFF: Listen, it's a game. Just a stupid game. We go, we play,
29   we leave.
30 TOM: No, Jeff. You go, you play — and not very well — and
31   you leave. The rest of us take it a little more seriously
32   than that.
33 JEFF: Maybe that's the problem right there. You guys take it
34   too seriously. It's only a *game*. It's not real life.
35 KEVIN: Isn't it? You don't join in at all. You do that in football,

1   you do that in life. You do a half-assed job and then walk
2   away from it like it means nothing. You should either
3   give one hundred per cent or quit.
4   JEFF: Just because I don't party with the guys doesn't mean
5   I don't give one hundred per cent.
6   TOM: We're not talking about partying. Football is a team
7   sport. If we don't all work as a team, we lose.
8   JEFF: So, here you go again. We lose because of me.
9   KEVIN: Well, we sure aren't winning because of you.
10   JEFF: Maybe you're right. Maybe I should quit.
11   TOM: The sad thing is, I don't think it would bother you at all.
12   Quitting would have no effect on you whatsoever.
13   JEFF: Like Kevin said, it's only a game.
14   KEVIN: I feel really sorry for you.
15   JEFF: Don't waste your pity on me. See you around, pal.
16   TOM: Not for a while. Kevin and I will be at practice. What
17   will you be doing?
18   JEFF: I'll watch the game. And I'll wait to see if you all *bond*
19   better without me around.
20   KEVIN: It's not without you around. Face it, you haven't been
21   around. You've been on the field, but you haven't been
22   with us.
23   TOM: Before you quit, you better think it over. Once you tell
24   the coach you're off the team, that's it. And I think it
25   means more to you than you are willing to admit.
26   JEFF: I bet you'd like to think that. See ya around. *(He exits.)*
27   TOM: He's going to regret quitting.
28   KEVIN: Do you really think so? I don't. I honestly don't think
29   he cares one way or the other. Like he said, for him it's
30   just a game.
31   TOM: And he just quits. Loser.
32
33
34
35

1 # FRESHMAN YEAR

2

3 *NATHAN:* A very young freshman. *KENNY:* A sophomore, enters the

4   area looking for NATHAN.

5 *SETTING:* The scene opens as NATHAN enters, very upset, almost

6   in tears, however trying to conceal the fact. He is alone for a

7   moment and then KENNY enters, concerned for NATHAN.

8

9 KENNY: Nathan, are you all right?

10 NATHAN: I'm OK. Just leave me alone for a while, OK?

11 KENNY: What the hell happened in there?

12 NATHAN: I don't know. I was just standing there, talking to

13   everyone, and all of a sudden — bam — they jumped all

14   over me.

15 KENNY: What did you say to them?

16 NATHAN: Nothing.

17 KENNY: You must have said something.

18 NATHAN: I swear, I didn't say anything. We were all just

19   hanging around, everyone was laughing and talking, I

20   made a comment and before I knew what happened,

21   Andrew, Darrin, even Margaret, were all yelling at me.

22 KENNY: You must have said something.

23 NATHAN: I don't know what.

24 KENNY: What were they talking about?

25 NATHAN: That's the stupid part. They weren't really talking

26   about anything. Just b.s.ing, you know. About school and

27   classes and teachers. Andrew said something about his

28   English class and I told him that if he needed help with

29   it, I'd be happy to work with him.

30 KENNY: Oh, boy.

31 NATHAN: What? What's oh, boy?

32 KENNY: You just don't know when to shut up, do you? Why

33   can't you just stand and listen to a conversation without

34   having to add your two cents?

35 NATHAN: What? I'm not allowed to speak?

1　KENNY:　Nathan, you're only a freshman. Andrew, Darrin,
2　　　　and Margaret are all seniors.
3　NATHAN:　So? I'm a freshman so I'm nothing?
4　KENNY:　Pretty much sums it up, yes. Freshmen shouldn't
5　　　　pop off.
6　NATHAN:　Pop off? I was offering my help with a class.
7　KENNY:　You're a freshman, Nathan. A freshman. That is the
8　　　　lowest of the low on the evolutionary scale in high school.
9　NATHAN:　I was trying to be nice.
10　KENNY:　Nice? How do you think it made Andrew feel to have
11　　　　some little pop-off freshman boy who hasn't even hit
12　　　　puberty yet offer assistance with a senior level English
13　　　　class?
14　NATHAN:　What's the big deal? I'm in Honors. That so-called
15　　　　senior level English class he's taking is doing the same
16　　　　work we're doing in Honors freshman English. I told him
17　　　　that . . .
18　KENNY:　In front of everyone?
19　NATHAN:　I was standing right there. I figured I was part of
20　　　　the conversation.
21　KENNY:　Idiot. Just standing in the general vicinity of speaking
22　　　　seniors does not give you license to contribute to their
23　　　　conversation.
24　NATHAN:　I don't get it.
25　KENNY:　You are a freshman, Nathan. A freshman. You are
26　　　　nothing. You will remain nothing, at least to the seniors,
27　　　　until the day they graduate.
28　NATHAN:　Well, then to Andrew I'll be nothing for an extra
29　　　　year if he doesn't get help in his English class.
30　KENNY:　See, that's what I mean. You need to learn to shut up.
31　　　　You're always coming up with these little smart-ass
32　　　　remarks that only get you in trouble.
33　NATHAN:　You're always doing it, too. How come you can do
34　　　　it and no one gets mad at you?
35　KENNY:　True, I have many friends among the upper class

1   kids. But that is because I am funny. You are just a pop

2   off. An annoying, self-centered pop off. Or at least, that's

3   how you come off.

4   NATHAN: For trying to help . . .

5   KENNY: You see it as trying to help . . .

6   NATHAN: That's all it was, helping a friend.

7   KENNY: You just don't get it. These guys are not your friends.

8   They're your sister's friends, not yours.

9   NATHAN: OK, I was helping my sister's friend, then. Big deal.

10   KENNY: You see it as trying to help. They see it as another

11   desperate attempt to fit in with people who don't want

12   you around.

13   NATHAN: What do you mean they don't want me around?

14   KENNY: They don't. You're always making some off-the-wall

15   comment, trying to be funny or something, and you just

16   end up bugging them.

17   NATHAN: Why is it all right for you to make comments?

18   KENNY: It's just different.

19   NATHAN: Why? What's so different?

20   KENNY: Probably the fact that because I don't care if they

21   like me or not. I have my own friends; I don't need them.

22   Every time you open your mouth whatever comes out

23   sounds stupid and annoying, at least to them.

24   NATHAN: Even to my own sister?

25   KENNY: Especially to your own sister. You think she enjoys

26   that every time she wants to hang out with her friends,

27   she turns around and there you are?

28   NATHAN: She drives me here, we go to the same school, it's

29   not that big a place. We're bound to run into each other.

30   KENNY: Tell me, what exactly happened back there when

31   you offered your help to Andrew on that English

32   assignment?

33   NATHAN: Nothing . . .

34   KENNY: Don't tell me nothing. I don't come out here and find

35   you almost in tears over nothing.

1   NATHAN: All I did was tell Andrew he could use my paper for
2   his assignment. Before I knew it, Margaret, my own flesh
3   and blood, was telling me to shut up, that Andrew didn't
4   need my help and to "get the hell out."
5   KENNY: What did Andrew say?
6   NATHAN: Nothing. He just looked at me and walked away.
7   Darrin told me that I should learn to keep my mouth
8   shut. He also told me that if I wasn't Margaret's brother
9   he would have punched me out a month ago.
10 KENNY: And you don't know why they are mad?
11 NATHAN: I guess. I don't know. I still don't see what the big
12 deal is.
13 KENNY: OK, listen — I'm going to help you out.
14 NATHAN: Help me out? How? Why?
15 KENNY: Why? Because I'm a nice guy. How? From now on,
16 before you open your mouth around those guys, you look
17 at me. If I raise my right index finger that means shut
18 up. If I raise my left thumb, that means shut up.
19 NATHAN: OK . . . hey, they both mean shut up. When do I
20 speak?
21 KENNY: Think about it.
22 NATHAN: . . . oh.
23 KENNY: Nathan, I like you. You're kind of a jerk sometimes,
24 but you'll grow out of it. I hope you'll listen to me and
25 take my advice. Otherwise, you are going to find yourself
26 sitting alone at lunch, at break, and pretty much having
27 no friends at all.
28 NATHAN: So, I just have to shut up?
29 KENNY: That and not try so hard to be everyone's friend. If
30 people like you, then they like you. If they don't, the hell
31 with them.
32 NATHAN: And that works for you?
33 KENNY: To be honest, it was kind of hard at first. But I began
34 to realize that sometimes someone, for whatever reason,
35 is just not going to like me, no matter how hard I try. And

127

1   it seems like the harder you try, the less they like you.
2 NATHAN: I see what you mean.
3 KENNY: So, after practice, you want to go to Rudy's?
4 NATHAN: OK. But wait here a minute.
5 KENNY: Where are you going?
6 NATHAN: To apologize to Andrew for embarrassing him
7   about that English assignment.
8 KENNY: No, Nathan. That would be worse. The last thing he
9   needs is an apology from a freshman about an assignment
10   he needs help with.
11 NATHAN: So, I should just keep my mouth shut?
12 KENNY: Now he's beginning to get the idea.
13 NATHAN: What about Darrin?
14 KENNY: Forget it. Darrin's a jerk. No matter what you do,
15   he'll never like you. No loss. The guy's a moron.
16 NATHAN: Oh, good. I thought I was the only one who noticed
17   that.
18 KENNY: Nah. We all think so. So, you ready to go back in?
19 NATHAN: Yeah.
20 KENNY: Now, what are you going to do when we go back in?
21 NATHAN: I'm going to keep my mouth shut.
22 KENNY: OK. You might make it through your freshman year
23   alive after all.
24
25
26
27
28
29
30
31
32
33
34
35

1 # THE WAITING GAME
2
3 ***RON, MARK, TODD, DAVID, ADAM:***   All in high school, getting
4   ready for a wild weekend together.
5 ***SETTING:***   Outdoor basketball court.
6
7 **MARK:**   *(Enters, looks around, sees he's alone. Dribbles basketball*
8   *for a moment or two, begins to narrate game.)* **Mark Avery**
9   **arrives center court. The crowd cheers their beloved**
10   **hero. Mark, humble guy that he is, waves to the admiring**
11   **hordes. The tip off! Mark takes the ball! The man is**
12   **unstoppable! He dodges, he moves, he drives down the**
13   **court. He shoots! It's in! The crowd roars. Mark is the**
14   **king! Mark is the king!** *(He looks over to see RON watching*
15   *him.)* **Hey, shoot some hoops, loser?**
16 **RON:**   Not now, butthead. I've got a date with your mother.
17 **MARK:**   Where are the guys?
18 **RON:**   I don't know. Adam said he'd be here as soon as he got
19   off work. David had to go to church. *(They both laugh.)*
20 **MARK:**   His parents still got him doing that, huh?
21 **RON:**   Yep. Some guys never grow up.
22 **MARK:**   What about Todd?
23 **TODD:**   *(Entering)* **What about me? I'm here, got the beer, and**
24   **you are queer.** *(He laughs at his joke.)*
25 **RON:**   That's funny. That's what Tiffany said last night about
26   you after your date when she came over to my house for
27   a handful of real man.
28 **TODD:**   And that's about all there is . . . a handful. Where's
29   David?
30 **MARK:**   Still off being holy.
31 **TODD:**   I can't believe his parents are still making him do this
32   church thing.
33 **RON:**   Hey, the guy has no choice. They drive him there, wait
34   till it's over and then take him home. It's not like he can
35   sneak out.

1   **MARK:**   Yeah, he has to wait until he's home and his parents
2   are asleep. That's when he can sneak out.
3   **DAVID:**   *(Entering on the run)* **I made it! Thanks for not leaving**
4   **without me, guys. I thought my parents would never go**
5   **to sleep.**
6   **TODD:**   I thought you were going to call Adam and he was
7   going to come get you on the corner.
8   **DAVID:**   I waited for him. The jerk never showed up.
9   **RON:**   Well, I don't feel like waiting around forever. He
10   doesn't show up in five minutes, I say we leave without
11   him.
12   **MARK:**   You forget, he's the one with the car.
13   **RON:**   So, we go find him, kick his butt, take his car and head
14   for Palm Springs without him. Hand me a beer, Toddy.
15   I need to be ready for the evening.
16   **ADAM:**   *(Entering)* **OK, big man, who's butt is going to get**
17   **kicked?**
18   **RON:**   Yours. Soon as I'm done with my beer, or two or three.
19   **DAVID:**   Thanks a lot for coming to get me, pal.
20   **MARK:**   What took you so long?
21   **TODD:**   Just for being late, you get your own beer.
22   **ADAM:**   Like I wouldn't have to anyway. Losers. I had to work
23   late. I, unlike you morons, have responsibilities to cover.
24   I have to pay for my car upkeep.
25   **RON:**   Ooohhh, poor baby. You have to put in a few dollars of
26   gas a week.
27   **MARK:**   Correct me if I'm wrong, butthead, but don't Mommy
28   and Daddy pay for insurance, repairs, payments? The list
29   goes on.
30   **ADAM:**   Who do you think has to pay for the gas to keep the
31   Adamobile on the road? And, hey, before any of you fools
32   get in my car, I want gas money.
33   **TODD:**   And what's fair about this?! You're the one with the
34   money, why should we have to pay you for gas?
35   **ADAM:**   Because I'm the one with the job.

1   **DAVID:**   **Tough job. You go to Daddy's office and turn out the**
2   **lights and lock up.**
3   **ADAM:**   **Hey, there's more to it than that. I have to make sure**
4   **the coffee timer is on too!** *(He laughs.)* **Pay up, parasites.**
5   **TODD:**   **I brought the beer. I don't have to pay.**
6   **ADAM:**   **That's fair.** *(He turns to the other three.)* **Guys? Your**
7   **coach awaits, but you don't enter until I see the green,**
8   **green cash of home.**
9   **MARK:**   **I shouldn't have to pay. This whole thing was my**
10   **idea. I set everything up. I made the hotel reservation. I**
11   **made sure that we'd all meet at the appointed time.**
12   **ADAM:**   **Tough. Pay up.**
13   **MARK:**   **Who's going to pay my phone bill?**
14   **ADAM:**   **I care? No. Pay up or no ride.**
15   **MARK:**   **What a jerk.**
16   **ADAM:**   **Ron? Cash please.**
17   **RON:**   **I shouldn't have to pay. Just the pleasure of my**
18   **company should be payment enough.**
19   **TODD:**   **Charge him double.**
20   **RON:**   **All right, all right. Gimme another beer.**
21   **DAVID:**   *(Reluctantly pulling out his wallet)* **It's not fair. You**
22   **have more money than all of us put together. Why should**
23   **we have to pay you?**
24   **ADAM:**   **You know what they say: The rich get richer, the poor**
25   **get — what was it again, Mark? Is it** *children?*
26   **MARK:**   *(There is a moment of tension.)* **I thought I told you not**
27   **to bring that up, Adam.**
28   **RON:**   **Lighten up, Mark. It's not like we don't all know about**
29   **you and Janna.**
30   **MARK:**   **I told you I don't want to talk about it, OK?**
31   **DAVID:**   **What?**
32   **TODD:**   **Mark, my man, you need a beer. Trust me, it will make**
33   **it all better; it always does.**
34   **ADAM:**   **I believe that was how he got into the mess originally.**
35   **DAVID:**   **What mess?**

1   **MARK:**   **Gimme that beer.** *(He downs the whole thing.)* **Hey! Let's**
2   **shoot some hoops for awhile.** *(He passes the ball to RON,*
3   *who fakes TODD, turns for the shot.)*
4   **RON:**   **Fakes him** *out of his jock!*
5   **DAVID:**   *(Stepping in, grabs the ball.)* **What are you guys talking**
6   **about?**
7   **RON:**   **You've never heard the phrase "faked out of his jock"?**
8   **David, David, David. Come into the world of sports, my**
9   **young friend.**
10   **DAVID:**   **What is going on?**
11   **ADAM:**   **Well, it seems that young Mr. Avery did the dirty deed**
12   **with the once innocent Janna Preston. And, being of**
13   **unsound mind and even unsounder moral standing,**
14   **allowed himself to be swayed by something other than**
15   **common sense. Which ultimately resulted in the**
16   **impending fatherhood he is now waiting to hear about.**
17   **MARK:**   *(Trying to change the subject)* **I don't know about you**
18   **guys, but I'm ready to hit the road.**
19   **RON:**   **And, beyond that, our good friend Mark has decided to**
20   **wait out the answer as far away from the lovely Janna**
21   **as possible.**
22   **TODD:**   **He has chosen to spend this time waiting with us,**
23   **his lifelong friends.**
24   **DAVID:**   **And when were you going to tell me? Why am I the**
25   **last to know?**
26   **MARK:**   **I didn't realize I had to clear my social calendar with**
27   **you, Dave. Next time I knock somebody up, I will give**
28   **you a call, OK?**
29   **DAVID:**   **I just think you should have told me, is all.**
30   **MARK:**   **Are we going or are we staying?**
31   **RON:**   *(Feeling no worse the wear for the three beers he's had. Not*
32   *sloppy, but buzzed)* **I'm ready. I've been ready. Man, I was**
33   **born ready. Palm Springs, spring break, break-fast, fast**
34   **women, women and me. Ah, free association. My therapist**
35   **would be so proud.**

1 DAVID: Wait a minute. You mean Janna Preston, the
2   sophomore?
3 MARK: David, I said that I was done talking about this, OK?
4 DAVID: It is Janna Preston, the sophomore. I didn't know
5   you were going with her.
6 RON: *(Bursting out with a laugh)* He's not going with her. He
7   *went* with her is about all.
8 ADAM: It's the old story: The popular senior takes advantage
9   of the insecure sophomore yearning for popularity.
10 TODD: *(Jumping into the story)* She sees him from across a
11   crowded room. He waves. "Is that Mark Avery?" she
12   whispers to a friend.
13 RON: *(Taking up the cue)* It's him. It's Mark. The Mark Avery.
14   The one and only captain of the football team.
15 ADAM: Senior class vice president.
16 TODD: Mr. B.M.O.C.
17 RON: And he waved at me! *(He swoons.)* Me!
18 ADAM: *(Narrating)* Sensing easy prey, Mark maneuvers over
19   to the unsuspecting innocent.
20 TODD: Hey, baby — he doesn't know her name yet — Hey,
21   baby.
22 RON: *(All aflutter)* Yes?
23 TODD: You're beautiful, baby. The best-looking chick in the
24   room.
25 RON: *(Batting eyelashes)* Oh, really, do you think so?
26 TODD: Whaddya say we make like a tree and get out of here?
27 RON: Oh, Mark, you're so clever.
28 TODD: *(Putting his arm around RON)* Come on, baby, I'll take
29   you to a real party. By the way, what's your name? *(TODD,*
30   *ADAM and RON are laughing uproariously at their cleverness.)*
31 DAVID: *(Looking at MARK who is not amused)* Is that what
32   happened?
33 MARK: Hey, she was cute. I thought she would be fun. I
34   didn't know what would happen. One thing led . . .
35 DAVID: Yeah, one thing led to another. Janna is my sister's

1   best friend.

2 MARK: Oh?

3 DAVID: I've known her since she was five years old.

4 TODD: Well, I guess Mark knows her a little better than you,
5   huh?

6 DAVID: This isn't funny, guys. I can't believe you are laughing
7   about this.

8 ADAM: Back off, David. You'd be laughing, too, if she was just
9   some girl.

10 TODD: And that's all she is. Some girl.

11 DAVID: She's a friend.

12 RON: No, David, Mr. I-just-got-out-of-church-and-still-have-
13   some-holiness-to-wipe-off-my-shoulders, to Mark at the
14   time she was just another girl willing to pay the price to
15   be with the most popular guy on campus.

16 MARK: I didn't put a gun to her head, you know.

17 DAVID: No, you just took advantage of the situation.

18 ADAM: And you are going to stand there and tell us that you
19   haven't done the same thing.

20 DAVID: She's a little girl.

21 MARK: Yeah, well.

22 DAVID: What are you going to do?

23 TODD: Why are you asking him? It's not his problem.

24 MARK: Todd, I'm not a complete jerk. I told her that if she
25   was in trouble, I'd take care of it.

26 RON: You gonna marry her?

27 MARK: *Hell no!* I said I'd take care of it. You know, help her
28   find a doctor in a clinic somewhere, drive her there, make
29   sure she's OK. You know.

30 DAVID: Mark! She's a little girl.

31 ADAM: Not so little as to not get herself in this mess. Hey,
32   David, face it. She took grown-up actions, and now she
33   has to take grown-up responsibilities.

34 MARK: And I said I'd help. For God's sake, I said I'd take care
35   of it. How the hell do you think I feel?

1   DAVID: Maybe you should have thought of this before.
2   RON: Have any of us? I mean, really, have any of us? Think
3   about it, David. When you were going with Julie, did you
4   even think about it? No, you didn't.
5   DAVID: She was on the pill.
6   TODD: That's what she told you. You don't know for sure. It
7   could be you in this situation, you know?
8   ADAM: Just because a girl says she's on the pill, you can
9   never be sure. Ever. Caution, my friends. Caution is what
10   I advise.
11   RON: I have chosen abstinence. *(He raises the glass in a toast to*
12   *himself.)* I am waiting.
13   MARK: Yeah, right, Ron. Waiting. Sure.
14   RON: I am. I never told you guys this, but when I was going
15   with Laurie, we had a little scare there for a while. Thank
16   God that's all it was, but it did the trick for me. I'm not
17   taking any chances.
18   TODD: You can honestly say that you're going to "wait"?
19   RON: Yep. At least for a while, till I'm old enough to take care
20   of any "problems" that may arise. I look at ole Mark over
21   there and think, there but for the grace of God go any
22   one of us.
23   MARK: *(Seeing them all look at him)* What are you looking at?
24   *(They don't answer, they just look.)* Stop it. Just knock it off.
25   I don't need your pity. She's probably not even pregnant,
26   anyway.
27   ADAM: When do you find out?
28   MARK: Pretty soon. She says she's a little late, but that
29   happens with tension and stuff, you know.
30   DAVID: And she is pretty young.
31   MARK: Shut up, David, OK? I've heard enough from you.
32   DAVID: Yeah. Great.
33   MARK: Listen, I'm ready to go. I need one night of blind fun.
34   Of not worrying about the future. Of just being with the
35   guys and being a fool.

1   **ADAM:**   **And who better than us to provide this. Gentlemen,**
2   **our chariot awaits.**
3   **TODD:**   **We need more beer. Ron drank it all.**
4   **ADAM:**   **No open containers in the car. It's against the law.**
5   **RON:**   **Hell, Adam, it's against the law for us to even drink.**
6   **What's wrong with breaking one law and not the other.**
7   **What an idiot.** *(They exit leaving MARK and DAVID on-stage.)*
8   **MARK:**   *(Looking at DAVID)* **You comin'?**
9   **DAVID:**   **You are one cold bastard sometimes, you know that,**
10   **Mark?**
11   **MARK:**   *(A little sadly)* **Yeah, I know. You comin'?**
12   **DAVID:**   **Yeah, I'm comin'.**
13
14
15
16
17
18
19
20
21
22
23
24
25
26
27
28
29
30
31
32
33
34
35

LOST IN SCHOOL

You know what I'm getting really tired of? People. Everyone always saying, "What's wrong?" "Why aren't you smiling?" "You've changed." How do they know I've changed? Maybe this is who I am and who they thought I was really didn't exist. Hey, take a look. This is it, guys. This is who I am. And if you can figure it out, you're doing a lot better than me.

Really, I don't know what's going on. I just don't feel like doing anything. I see my homework sitting on my desk. I really do try to sit down and do it... but I can't. I just can't. No, I don't *want* to. I just don't feel like it. I look at all my friends. Or at least people I thought were my friends. They don't really know me. They know who I let them know, but it isn't the real me. It's just what I let them see. But I'm tired of being that person.

I get frustrated, you know? I have all these things inside me, and they just can't get out. And I don't know why. People say it's a "phase" and I will grow out of it. But I don't think it is. This is it. My "phase" was before. What you see now is the real me. And it's scary. I've never been like this before. No one ever told me to smile, 'cause I always smiled. I was always happy. And now I'm not, and I don't even know why. It's not that I'm unhappy. I'm... I guess I'm nothing. That's what I feel like inside. Like there's this big hole inside of me and I can't fill it up. I'm not even mad about it. I'm just sort of "there."

You know what I dread? Lunch. You know why? Because I don't hang out with anybody. It's not like I'm one of those geeks that sit on the bricks in the quad, hoping not to be pelted by flying fruit remains. I've got plenty of people to hang with, but no specific ones. I just move from group to group, talking, laughing, and inside I'm wondering why I'm there. That's why I go off campus to lunch. It's an excuse not to be on the fringe

1   of a group. The funny thing is, if I told any of my friends, they
2   would just shake their heads and say, "Oh, there he goes,
3   trying to get attention." But it's really how I feel. Sort of like
4   a fish out of water. Think about it. It's not really a very funny
5   picture. A fish flops around on the sand, slowly suffocating,
6   hoping an ocean wave of life will bring him back into his own
7   world. Nine times out of ten the wave doesn't surge high
8   enough on the beach to save him. That's how I feel. Like I'm
9   waiting for a surge to bring me back to life . . . and the tide is
10   going out.
11
12
13
14
15
16
17
18
19
20
21
22
23
24
25
26
27
28
29
30
31
32
33
34
35

MICHAEL

I've always been lucky. That's just the way it's been for me. I do things and I never get caught. It's not like I'm a cheat or a schemer, it's just that I'm not a catcher. You know what I mean? Catcher. People that do stuff and always get caught. Like I was in this really bad car accident. Hey, totally my fault. I was flying down the freeway at about ninety. Now, here's the irony. My own car had broken down, so I had to take my parents' car that day. Normally they would *never* let me drive their car, but for some reason it just worked out that I did. Anyway, I'm driving ... really flying ... and all of a sudden I lost control of the car. Next thing I know I'm hanging upside down, the car's on its roof, but I'm OK. And why? Because my parents' car has those automatic seat belts. I *never* wear my seat belt, but I didn't have any choice this time because the car automatically puts them on you and locks them. So, for all intents and purposes, I should be dead. But I'm not.

Another example. OK, the last day of school I find out I don't have enough units to graduate. I'm like three units short. And the counselor is telling me all this with this happy little smirk on her face because she hates me anyway because I've gone through four years of high school doing things bad enough to make people crazy but not to get in real trouble. So, now she has me. And it's the last day of school so there is no way I can make up those three units. So I figure I finally am caught and how unfair it is. I mean, I am sitting in my car in the school parking lot crying like a baby, afraid to go home. After all, my father is an elementary school principal and this is going to be really tough on him. All of a sudden, *wham*, it hits me. She didn't count those night school units! I leap out of my car and fly down to the office. You should have seen the look on her face. Was she disappointed! So, I graduate. Again, I get the save.

1   Well, last night I . . . uh, *became a man,* if you get my drift.
2   It was with someone I really care about and she's only been
3   with one other guy. So, I didn't use a condom. I *know* I should
4   have, so don't lecture. But I was determined that my first time
5   would not be with a condom. But, for some reason, I have a
6   funny feeling inside. I mean, hey, it was great. Worth the wait,
7   everything I've heard and more. But I didn't use a condom.
8   And now that the afterglow is fading . . . I'm wondering if
9   maybe this time my luck has run out.
10
11
12
13
14
15
16
17
18
19
20
21
22
23
24
25
26
27
28
29
30
31
32
33
34
35

TONY

(TONY explains how he gets around his strict disciplinary parents.)
  My parents. What a comedy. You should see it sometimes. They try to get me angry. It's funny how they are. But I won't let them see how they make me feel. You see, that's the trick in it. Don't let 'em see how they make you feel. It makes them nuts. Like, last week. I come in late. Hey, I know I'm late. I'm seventeen. I can tell time. I know that punishment is imminent, but they have to make it like it's some big deal. OK, so they say, *(Imitating their voices)* "Son, you are grounded." Ha, what a shock, you know. So I say OK. Now here is the great part. I give them this little half smile. Not a smirk, you understand, because that would give them what they like to call "just cause." Then I'd really get it. No, just a little smile, sort of a Mona Lisa kind of thing. It just kills them. They don't know what the hell I'm thinking. So even though I get punished . . . I win.

CHAD

The day the cast was posted, I stood out by the theatre door, afraid to go in. Everyone was crowding around, waiting. It was in the morning, about 8:30. The sun was trying to come out, but the clouds were forcing it out of the sky. These big black clouds, just floating slowly, you know, like clouds do. I watched them for a minute and I could smell the rain. Remember that song from *The Fantasticks*? The one that goes, "Soon it's gonna rain, I can feel it. Soon it's gonna rain, I can tell?" Well, I can always tell when it's gonna rain. I don't even have to see that there are clouds. I can smell the wetness in the air. And that day, that cloudy, dark day with the sun waging a losing battle with the atmosphere, I waited with a bunch of other kids to see if I got a part in the show. There was this other guy, about my age, pacing and smoking a cigarette. I watched him pace and watched that trail of smoke wind its way up to join the other clouds and help block out my sun. He glanced over at me and gave me this tense smile. "Nerves," he said and pulled a long drag from his cigarette. He looked cool, though, in a very "with-it-part-of-the-in-crowd" sort of way. Right then the door opened and everyone rushed in to check the cast list. Mr. Cool Smoker Guy was dancing all around. Obviously he got the part he wanted. I looked up at the clouds and the sun. For just a moment the sun won the war and revealed itself full and glowing. I took that as a good sign and went in to check the cast list myself. Oh, I was there, all right. Chorus. Again. Well, at least I made it. I went back outside and the sun was shining fully, having burned the clouds away. I figured it was sort of like a natural spotlight meant just for me so everybody would know that, yet again, I was inadequate. No wonder I like the rain.

CASEY

(CASEY is explaining the feelings and memories brought on by discussing fathers with friends.)

     I have only one memory of my father still living at home. He left when I was very young, you know. It was late, not yet dark. Dusk, I guess. I don't know why I remember that so well. I can still see him framed by the light from the open door. And I could see the street lights had just come on. My mother was holding me, and the more they yelled, the tighter she held on. I had to have been very young, because I remember holding onto my bottle — not drinking from it — just holding it. The more they yelled, the tighter Mom held me and the tighter I held the bottle. Then quick like, he moved towards us. The light from the lamp was caught by the diamond ring he still wears on his right hand. I hate that ring. That hand flew through the light and slammed down. He hit my mother while she was holding me. This respected, well-known businessman hit a woman holding a child. Unbelievable. And still, I didn't cry. I sat on the floor next to my mother and she spoke. I can still hear the low, almost animal tone she used. "Get out. Go." And I remember I stood up and looked at my father and said very clearly, "Go." It was my first clear word. And our last conversation.

◆ MIXED ◆

WHY DO I EVEN BOTHER?

MARTIN: A 17-year-old young man, having a hard time with women.

JANICE: His best friend, because she asks nothing of him, except friendship.

SETTING: During the scene, the two are eating lunch together. As the scene opens, they are looking for a place to sit.

JANICE: I'm telling you Martin, the next time we go out to lunch, you better have money. I am getting real tired of picking up your slack.

MARTIN: I told you I would drive. I would think the least you could do is spend a few pennies on a lousy thirty-nine cent taco without complaining.

JANICE: It wouldn't be so bad if you were the one eating the thirty-nine cent taco. But no, it's me, because that is all I have left after you order your macho nachos, super burrito and jumbo supreme taco.

MARTIN: Hey, I'm a growing boy.

JANICE: No kidding. Take a look at that gut.

MARTIN: *(Hitting himself on the stomach)* Flat and as hard as a rock.

JANICE: Not unlike your head. *(They sit down and begin to eat.)* And this time, I don't want to see the food dripping out of your mouth, OK?

MARTIN: Fine.

JANICE: Also, try to taste your food at least once before you inhale it. You could be eating sawdust and not know it.

MARTIN: Fine. Geez, what's your problem?

JANICE: Nothing. I just get a little annoyed spending all this money watching you devour food you don't even taste ... until perhaps later when you lick it off your chin.

MARTIN: Whatever, Janice. Hey, give me a sip of your coke.

JANICE: That's another thing. Why don't you order your own

1   damn coke?

2   MARTIN: Because it's all you can drink, and I can drink all

3   of yours and you can fill it back up. See, I'm thinking all

4   the time, trying to save you money.

5   JANICE: Oh, gee, thanks so much. How considerate.

6   MARTIN: All part of that Turner mystique.

7   JANICE: You know, you do have a certain charm. I don't

8   know what it is, but you do have a certain . . . I don't

9   know . . .

10   MARTIN: Charisma? Magnetism? Allure?

11   JANICE: I don't know, but whatever it is, it grows on you . . .

12   MARTIN: Oh, yeah?

13   JANICE: Like a fungus.

14   MARTIN: Great. Thanks a lot.

15   JANICE: No problem. *(They eat silently for a moment.)*

16   MARTIN: Aren't you even going to ask?

17   JANICE: Ask what?

18   MARTIN: Why I wanted you to go to lunch with me today?

19   JANICE: I figured you needed someone to pay for you.

20   MARTIN: Janice, I'm being serious.

21   JANICE: Martin, so am I.

22   MARTIN: I need to talk to you as a woman.

23   JANICE: Hard to do, since you aren't one.

24   MARTIN: I mean, you as a woman.

25   JANICE: I never knew you noticed.

26   MARTIN: Can we please be serious?

27   JANICE: OK. *(Putting her food down, folding her hands on the*

28   *table)* What?

29   MARTIN: Why can't I get girls?

30   JANICE: Oh . . . you are serious, aren't you?

31   MARTIN: I told you I was. I figured that you, being both a

32   woman and my best friend, would be completely honest

33   with me and tell me why I can't seem to get girls.

34   JANICE: Could it be because you are a jerk?

35   MARTIN: I can see you refuse to be serious about this.

1   JANICE: You are mistaken, Martin. I am being very serious.
2   You are an idiot. OK, at Suzanne's party last night, what
3   did you do?
4   MARTIN: See, that's the thing. I was with this one girl.
5   JANICE: What was her name?
6   MARTIN: I think it was Krissy or Missy or something.
7   JANICE: Point one.
8   MARTIN: What?
9   JANICE: I'll explain later.
10 MARTIN: Anyway, I was with this girl, and Brandon was with
11   this other chick. And by the end of the night, Brandon
12   was taking his chick home, and I am sitting alone with
13   my beer.
14 JANICE: And what happened when you were with Krissy or
15   Missy or whatever?
16 MARTIN: I was telling her about myself, and how I want to
17   be an actor and stuff.
18 JANICE: And were you drinking?
19 MARTIN: Well... *(JANICE gives him a "look.")* OK, I was
20   getting flopping drunk, but she was laughing. Everyone
21   was laughing. I'm a funny guy.
22 JANICE: So, you spend the night drinking and talking
23   about yourself, and you can't figure out why you end up
24   alone?
25 MARTIN: No.
26 JANICE: What a moron. Did you ever think to ask her about
27   herself?
28 MARTIN: I don't care about her — why would I ask?
29 JANICE: Then what are you complaining about?
30 MARTIN: I just want a little action. I'm seventeen, I'm primed.
31 JANICE: Why do I bother? You are the biggest waste of my
32   time.
33 MARTIN: No, come on, I need your help.
34 JANICE: First off, I am not going to help you "get a little
35   action." And second, you are a swine.

1   MARTIN: Just tell me what I'm doing wrong. And why does
2   Brandon get all these girls? He's just as big a swine as I
3   am.
4   JANICE: OK, I'll tell you. I don't know why, but I will. I
5   probably just pity you for the miserable little creature
6   you are.
7   MARTIN: I can accept that. So, what's the deal?
8   JANICE: The reason Brandon gets women is because he
9   makes them feel he is interested in them. He gets them
10   to talk about themselves and he at least pretends he is
11   interested.
12   MARTIN: But he isn't. All he wants is the same thing I do.
13   JANICE: The difference is, he makes them feel like they are
14   important, and because he looks them in the eye and
15   actually appears to be listening, women fall for him.
16   MARTIN: Listening, huh?
17   JANICE: And your drinking is another thing.
18   MARTIN: What about it? Brandon drinks.
19   JANICE: But does he get "flopping drunk"? *(MARTIN shakes*
20   *his head no.)* See? But, what is he doing when you are
21   drunk?
22   MARTIN: He's laughing. Everyone is. I told you, I'm funny.
23   JANICE: Right. He's laughing. He is sitting with a girl,
24   looking at you acting like a lush, falling all over yourself
25   and telling the girl that he apologizes for his drunken
26   friend. Which again makes him look sensitive.
27   MARTIN: But even that girl I was with last night was
28   laughing.
29   JANICE: Great. She's laughing at you falling down drunk
30   and going home with someone else. Need I say more?
31   MARTIN: So, I shouldn't drink?
32   JANICE: That would be a start.
33   MARTIN: And I should pretend I'm listening to her?
34   JANICE: Don't pretend, really listen.
35   MARTIN: Hey, I don't care what she says. You said Brandon

1   pretends, and the girls fall for it. I'm a better actor than
2   Brandon and you know it. I can be just as sensitive as
3   the next guy.
4 JANICE: Try being nice, too.
5 MARTIN: Nice?! How?
6 JANICE: Open doors, pay for something, be nice.
7 MARTIN: That's going a little far.
8 JANICE: Just do it, dammit. Be nice, you little worm.
9 MARTIN: God, calm down. OK, I'll be nice. You really think
10   this will work?
11 JANICE: I hope not. But it probably will. I don't know why I
12   bother to try and help you.
13 MARTIN: Because you're my best friend in the whole world
14   and you love me.
15 JANICE: Sad, but true. A sorry state of affairs, isn't it?
16 MARTIN: I'd do the same for you.
17 JANICE: But I don't need help. I have a boyfriend.
18 MARTIN: Well, I don't want a girlfriend. I just want a little ...
19 JANICE: I know, action. *(She looks upward.)* Please, God,
20   forgive me for helping him. I think I've betrayed women
21   everywhere.
22 MARTIN: OK, Kelly's party is tonight. I'll try out this
23   sensitive crap stuff then. *(He gets up, leaving the remnants*
24   *of lunch on the table, and exits.)*
25 JANICE: *(Picking up the trash, watching him exit)* Why do I even
26   bother? *(Calling after him)* Disgusting pig!
27 MARTIN: *(Calling back)* But a sensitive one!
28
29
30
31
32
33
34
35

1 # IN OTHER WORDS
2
3   *HE:*   Verbose, sure of himself, ready to impress at all costs.
4   **SHE:**   Translates for her friend. She's used to it; it doesn't faze her
5   at all.
6   **SETTING:**   Scene takes place as HE and SHE approach the teacher,
7   asking for a test to be postponed to a later day. Unless otherwise
8   noted, HE and SHE talk directly to the teacher. They can
9   respond to one another with looks, but each must immediately
10   pick up on each other's cues.
11
12   HE: **I would hope that I am not intruding into your private**
13   **space, because I know as a fellow human being that we**
14   **all value our own solitary cosmos.**
15   SHE: **Are you busy?**
16   HE: **You see, there exists at this point in time a situation that**
17   **troubles me down to the deepest resources of my soul.**
18   SHE: **I have a problem.**
19   HE: **This ...** *(Searches for the right word.)*
20   SHE: **Problem.**
21   HE: *(To SHE)* **Thanks ever so.** *(SHE simply nods.)* **This** *problem*
22   **involves and includes my peers who seek to share in the**
23   **vast expanse of knowledge you are endeavoring to impart**
24   **to us.**
25   SHE: **Some of us have a question.**
26   HE: **To put it simply, some of us have a question.**
27   SHE: *(To HE)* **I just said that.**
28   HE: *(To SHE)* **You did?**
29   SHE: *(To HE)* **Uh-huh.**
30   HE: *(To SHE)* **Oh. Abject apologies.**
31   SHE: *(To HE)* **Sure.**
32   HE: **As I was saying, myself and my peers, and might I add we**
33   **all sit in awe at your intellectual prowess ...**
34   SHE: **You're pretty smart, so ...**
35   HE: **Perhaps, if we could take this time to communicate on a**

1   level that would explore the facts of this dilemma, we would
2   be able, as a team you see, to slowly but surely draw ourselves
3   out of this murky quandary that has so bedeviled us.
4 SHE: Can we talk?
5 HE: You see, my contemporaries, my counterparts if you will,
6   are befuddled by this ...
7 SHE: Problem.
8 HE: OK, for lack of a better word, *problem.*
9 SHE: *(To HE)* It's a good word.
10 HE: *(To SHE)* But so limiting in its meaning.
11 SHE: *(To HE)* I think it's pretty clear.
12 HE: OK, problem.
13 SHE: That's what I thought.
14 HE: This *problem* has us all a tad concerned about the
15   ultimate outcome of the concept that you have asked us
16   to attack.
17 SHE: We don't get it.
18 HE: What we are trying to say is that this particular moment
19   in time has inextricably brought us to the impasse we
20   now encounter within this educational situation.
21 SHE: This test is hard.
22 HE: So, what I hypothesize at this twinkling of a moment is
23   that, if given proper counsel, our destiny ... nay our fate,
24   our kismet if you will, would be better served if you would
25   perhaps, in your all encompassing wisdom, would
26   consider deferring this surprise, although worthy,
27   examination.
28 SHE: We're not ready for the test.
29 HE: Now, please, I beg of you to understand that this is not a
30   reflection whatsoever upon your skills as an educator.
31 SHE: We didn't study.
32 HE: Nor, may I add, is it a comment upon your rights to make
33   any inquiry you would choose to indulge in as to our
34   comprehension of the materials you have so brilliantly
35   covered in class.

1   SHE: We didn't study.
2   HE: However, the fact remains, and irretrievably so, that
3   impending proof of our own inadequacy looms before us
4   in an ugly and despicable shadow.
5   SHE: We're gonna fail.
6   HE: So, I come to you abject in my heartfelt apologies.
7   SHE: Sorry, really we are.
8   HE: And I supplicate myself before you to please reconsider
9   the moment at hand and reverse yourself in this horrific
10   episode that we are about to traverse.
11 SHE: We're just not ready for a test.
12 HE: I pledge to you a sacred vow that you will not be disap-
13   pointed if you answer in the affirmative.
14 SHE: Please say yes.
15 HE: We await your response with bated breath and hearts
16   aflutter with anticipation.
17 SHE: So, whaddaya say?
18 HE: May we, if at all possible, defer this inevitable investi-
19   gation into our accumulated knowledge until the sun
20   arises upon a dewy new day, one filled with renewed
21   hope for a better future?
22 SHE: Can we take the test tomorrow?
23 HE: The forthcoming evening shall be spent in contemplative
24   analysis, examination, and probing into the field of study
25   that we need to more fully explore in order to be more
26   well versed in the area of concern.
27 SHE: We're gonna study all night.
28 HE: You will not be disappointed.
29 SHE: No way.
30 BOTH: Please give us the test tomorrow. *(They happily react to*
31   *the "yes" that is given them, then respond.)*
32 HE: Emotionally, I lay myself bare before you and humbly
33   proffer my heartfelt gratitude at your answer.
34 SHE: Thank you.
35

HOW OLD ARE YOU?

MICHELLE: Age 17, a senior looking for a boyfriend.

STEVE: Age 14, but looks older. Well built.

SETTING: MICHELLE and STEVE are standing outside the counseling office on the first day of school waiting to change their schedules.

MICHELLE: *(Looking through the window)* **Dammit. I can't believe this.** *(She looks over and notices STEVE. She smiles.)* **Hi.**

STEVE: *(Looking up from his own scheduling problems, he smiles back.)* **Hi.**

MICHELLE: **Long wait, huh?**

STEVE: **Yeah.**

MICHELLE: **You have many classes to switch?**

STEVE: **No, just one. I need to take sports during sixth period, so I have to move my science class to the morning.**

MICHELLE: **Probably a good idea. I mean switching.**

STEVE: **I guess so.**

MICHELLE: **No, I mean because you'll be more awake in the morning so you can pay attention in the science class.**

STEVE: **Yeah.** *(They chuckle a little.)* **So . . .**

MICHELLE: **Yes?**

STEVE: **Nothing.**

MICHELLE: **You're new, aren't you?**

STEVE: **Yes.**

MICHELLE: **My name's Michelle.**

STEVE: **Mine's Steve.**

MICHELLE: **Where did you go before?**

STEVE: **Nowhere around here. We just moved over the summer. I used to live in Maryland.**

MICHELLE: **Maryland. How exciting. Isn't that where they make syrup?**

STEVE: **No, I think that's Vermont.**

155

1   MICHELLE: That's right. *(A little embarrassed)* **Silly me.**

2   STEVE: Have you always lived here?

3   MICHELLE: Oh, yeah. Been with the same kids forever.

4   STEVE: That must be nice. My dad's in the army, so we've

5   moved quite a lot.

6   MICHELLE: Really? Like where?

7   STEVE: A lot of places. Most places we lived for only six

8   months or a year, except for Germany. We lived there

9   four years.

10   MICHELLE: Germany. Wow. Did you get to travel a lot?

11   STEVE: Oh, yeah. Especially because of sports. You know

12   how here you travel on a bus to play the next town? Well

13   in Europe, you travel on a train to play the next country.

14   MICHELLE: What a great life.

15   STEVE: It was OK.

16   MICHELLE: *(Really looking at him)* So, with that great body, I

17   bet you are a swimmer.

18   STEVE: Pretty much all sports. Tennis, wrestling, football,

19   and swimming. There's no TV to speak of in Germany, at

20   least not like here, so I didn't have a choice. Sports or

21   solitude.

22   MICHELLE: I bet you have quite a bit of experience . . . in

23   life.

24   STEVE: I guess.

25   MICHELLE: You know, we'll probably be seeing a lot of each

26   other. I'm a varsity cheerleader, so I go to everything.

27   I'm also in ASB.

28   STEVE: ASB?

29   MICHELLE: Student government. We plan things for the

30   school and get the spirit going and . . . well, you know,

31   that kind of stuff.

32   STEVE: Oh, I see. Sounds like fun.

33   MICHELLE: You ought to see if you could fit it in your

34   schedule.

35   STEVE: I don't think I'd have time. You know, being new and

1   all, I don't want to overdo myself.

2   MICHELLE: That's probably a good idea.

3   STEVE: Yep. *(There is a moment or two of silence. STEVE smiles,*

4   *looks back at his schedule. MICHELLE looks him up and down,*

5   *thinking.)*

6   MICHELLE: I bet it was hard leaving Maryland and all your

7   friends.

8   STEVE: Like I said, I was only there six months.

9   MICHELLE: I'm sure you had a girlfriend. It must have been

10   hard to leave her.

11   STEVE: *(A little shy)* No, no girlfriend.

12   MICHELLE: *(Quite pleased)* Oh, what a shame. *(Catching*

13   *herself)* I mean what a shame.

14   STEVE: It should be different here, though.

15   MICHELLE: *(Moving in on him)* Oh, why?

16   STEVE: Well, my dad retired from the service, so we are here

17   for good.

18   MICHELLE: How wonderful. You'll be here for the whole

19   year.

20   STEVE: Looks that way.

21   MICHELLE: Then I guess you'll need someone to show you

22   around, huh?

23   STEVE: It would be nice. I don't have a car yet, so I don't get

24   around much.

25   MICHELLE: No problem. I have a car. I would love to show

26   you around the city.

27   STEVE: You'd do that? Really?

28   MICHELLE: I'd love it. In fact, I know one place off the top of

29   my head that I could take you this weekend!

30   STEVE: Yeah? Where's that?

31   MICHELLE: The Back to School Dance. See, it's a tradition

32   here that the girls ask the guys to the first dance.

33   STEVE: A dance? I don't know . . .

34   MICHELLE: . . . How to dance? No problem. I'll teach you. I'm

35   sure that a great athlete like you would have no problem.

1   STEVE: It's not that. It's my parents.

2   MICHELLE: Your who?

3   STEVE: My parents. They really don't want me dating yet.

4   MICHELLE: You're not serious? *(He nods his head yes.)* **What?**

5   Are they expecting you to wait until college?

6   STEVE: They think I should be sixteen.

7   MICHELLE: Excuse me?

8   STEVE: They think I should be sixteen. They think I am too

9   young to start dating.

10   MICHELLE: How old are you?

11   STEVE: I'm fourteen. I'm a freshman.

12   MICHELLE: Excuse me?

13   STEVE: How old are you?

14   MICHELLE: I'll be eighteen in November. I'm a senior.

15   STEVE: You're kidding.

16   MICHELLE: A freshman. Great. I'm picking up on a freshman.

17   *(She looks him over.)* You don't look like a freshman.

18   STEVE: No? What do I look like?

19   MICHELLE: Never mind. I'm so embarrassed.

20   STEVE: Does this mean you don't want to show me around?

21   MICHELLE: No offense, Steve, but I couldn't. I mean . . .

22   you're a *freshman.* *(She shudders and looks around.)* You

23   won't tell anyone I asked you out, will you?

24   STEVE: So, all of a sudden you don't like me now?

25   MICHELLE: No, you're fine. It's just that, you know, a

26   freshman. I have a reputation to maintain. If I dated a

27   freshman I'd be dust.

28   STEVE: *(A little hurt)* Oh. I see. Hey, that's OK.

29   MICHELLE: I'm sorry, really. If I had known, I would have

30   never . . . but I mean . . . after all . . . well, look at that

31   body.

32   STEVE: Sports.

33   MICHELLE: I guess so! *(She keeps looking at him.)*

34   STEVE: It's no big deal. I understand.

35   MICHELLE: It's too bad you're so good looking.

1 **STEVE:** **Thanks.** *(He smiles.)*

2 **MICHELLE:** **My little sister might be interested in you.**

3 **STEVE:** **I'd still like to see you, though.**

4 **MICHELLE:** **Steve, I can't . . . at least not in public.**

5 **STEVE:** **What do you mean?**

6 **MICHELLE:** **I read somewhere that every boy should have**

7 **an older woman in his life at least once.**

8 **STEVE:** **Oh? And?**

9 **MICHELLE:** **I can't believe I am saying this. After we're done**

10 **here, do you want to go get something to eat?**

11 **STEVE:** **Sure.**

12 **MICHELLE:** **OK. And someday we'll look back on this with**

13 **fond memories, right?**

14 **STEVE:** **I'm sure I will.**

15 **MICHELLE:** **Steve, they won't be *that* fond.**

16 **STEVE:** **OK.**

17 **MICHELLE:** **OK. I can't believe I'm actually doing this.**

18 **STEVE:** *(Smiling at her)* **I can't either.**

19 **MICHELLE:** **What the heck, huh?**

20 **STEVE:** **Yeah.** *(They look at each other and smile.)*

21

22

23

24

25

26

27

28

29

30

31

32

33

34

35

LEGALITIES

ANN: Self-possessed young woman, able to take care of herself in any situation.

HENRY: Cocky, self-assured.

SETTING: ANN is sitting by herself in a secluded area. She looks up and sees HENRY approaching. With annoyance, she gathers her things and begins to leave.

HENRY: Hey, babe, *(He sits down next to her)* **what ya doin'?**

ANN: Not much. *(She stacks her books.)*

HENRY: Where you going?

ANN: Anywhere you're not.

HENRY: I sense a problem, babe. You mad at me?

ANN: Number one, my name is not "babe." Number two, I would have to have some sort of emotional attachment to you to be mad at you, so the answer to that question is no, I am not mad at you.

HENRY: Hey, why do you treat me like that? What? You too good for me?

ANN: I didn't say that, Henry. I just have to get going.

HENRY: You know what I've noticed? That every time we're alone, you can't seem to stand it. Why? Because your family has more money than mine?

ANN: Oh, yes. That's what it is. Everyone knows what a materialistic snob I am. See ya.

HENRY: Wait a minute. *(She stops and looks at him with a bored expression.)* **I want to know why you hate me.**

ANN: I never said I hated you.

HENRY: You don't have to say it. Everything you do shows it. You can't stand to be alone with me. You never talk to me except to ask me to get out of your way. You can barely make eye contact with me right now.

ANN: *(Looking at him directly)* **I have to leave, OK?**

HENRY: No, it's not OK. I want to know what the problem is.

160

1   **Every other girl on this campus would be thrilled to be**
2   **alone with me ...** *(He sees her roll her eyes.)* **I didn't mean**
3   **that the way it came out.**
4   **ANN:** Of course you didn't. Certainly. Is there anything else?
5   **HENRY:** **Dammit, Ann, I want to know what I ever did to you**
6   **that makes you so nasty and mean.** *(He tries sweet-talking*
7   *her.)* **Come on, you gotta admit, I'm kind of cute.** *(He flashes*
8   *a smile that he knows never fails.)*
9   **ANN:** **I never said you weren't cute.**
10   **HENRY:** **There you go ...**
11   **ANN:** **And I never said I hated you ...**
12   **HENRY:** **OK, we're making some progress here.**
13   **ANN:** **However, I don't like you.**
14   **HENRY:** **What? Why? What have I ever done to you? Ever?**
15   **ANN:** **Nothing.**
16   **HENRY:** **Oh, that's it. You've felt neglected by me.**
17   **ANN:** **Boy oh boy, there is just no end to that ego of yours, is**
18   **there? You think every girl in the world is just begging**
19   **to be by your side.**
20   **HENRY:** **Aren't they?** *(Smiles charmingly.)*
21   **ANN:** **You kid yourself. Not every girl in the world desires you.**
22   **HENRY:** **Not in the world ... just at this school.** *(ANN shakes*
23   *her head in disgust and begins to walk off. HENRY runs around in*
24   *front of her to cut her path.)* **Get a sense of humor. Can't you**
25   **see I'm kidding?**
26   **ANN:** **No, you're not. You really do think that. And you're**
27   **right. Most of the girls at this school would be thrilled to go**
28   **out with you ... so why don't you go ask them?**
29   **HENRY:** **Because you're the one I'm with right now. You're**
30   **the one I want to go out with.**
31   **ANN:** **Please. Give me a break. If I went out with you, you'd**
32   **have made your conquest and the thrill of the chase would**
33   **be over for you, then it would be adios, Ann.**
34   **HENRY:** **Oh, that's what it is. You're afraid if we went out, you'd**
35   **end up getting hurt.**

1   **ANN:**   No, because you have to care about someone for them
2   to hurt you.
3   **HENRY:**   You mean if I were lying bleeding in the street you
4   wouldn't come to my aid?
5   **ANN:**   I would do that for any dog . . .
6   **HENRY:**   Very funny . . .
7   **ANN:**   Listen, Henry, I have absolutely no interest in you, OK?
8   None. Zero. Look, what's in my hand? *(She holds out an*
9   *empty palm.)* Nothing, right? Well, that's how much I care
10   about you.
11   **HENRY:**   Jeez, you can be one cold woman.
12   **ANN:**   No, I can be one honest woman. Something you're
13   obviously not used to.
14   **HENRY:**   What if I told you we'd go someplace really special?
15   That it would be the date of a lifetime? The best food,
16   the best sights, the best time you ever had?
17   **ANN:**   I would tell you to save your money. Why are you doing
18   this? How much clearer do I have to be? Now, I am
19   leaving. I have places to go, people to see and things to do.
20   **HENRY:**   *(Getting a little angry)* I'm not done talking about this.
21   **ANN:**   *(Looking back at him)* I am.
22   **HENRY:**   *(Reaching out, grabbing her arm and turning her towards*
23   *him)* I said I wasn't.
24   **ANN:**   *(Not at all afraid)* Get your hands off me right now.
25   **HENRY:**   I said I wasn't done talking about this.
26   **ANN:**   If these Neanderthal tactics are supposed to impress
27   me, you have obviously misjudged who you are dealing
28   with.
29   **HENRY:**   Listen, I don't appreciate being treated like dirt.
30   **ANN:**   Then quit acting like dirt. I said to get your hands off me.
31   **HENRY:**   Not until you tell me what is so bad about me.
32   **ANN:**   I think we are seeing a pretty good display of it right
33   now.
34   **HENRY:**   *(Slightly shaking her)* You drove me to this.
35   **ANN:**   *(Pulling away from him)* I what? I *drove* you to this? So,

1   this is how you handle situations that don't go your way?

2   You get violent.

3   HENRY: Not always. Only when pushed.

4   ANN: So, is that why you roughed up that little freshman on

5   the first day of school?

6   HENRY: Hey, he just had to understand that he was a scrub.

7   He didn't get out of my way, so I dealt with it.

8   ANN: You're a joke, you know that? Just a joke. That little

9   guy isn't even fourteen years old, he's barely five feet tall.

10   But you had to "deal with him"?

11   HENRY: I handle things the way I see they need to be

12   handled.

13   ANN: Like me, right now?

14   HENRY: This is different. You are openly insulting me.

15   ANN: So, you think that makes it all right to touch me? What

16   gives you the right?

17   HENRY: You and your smart mouth, that's what. If you'd have

18   just shut that smart mouth, been nice and gone out with

19   me, we would have had a few laughs, you would have

20   had a great time, and that would have been that.

21   ANN: You really think you are some sort of prize, don't you?

22   Well, you're not. You're just another big mouth macho

23   guy who thinks because he's fairly good looking he can

24   do anything he wants and get away with it.

25   HENRY: So far, it's worked.

26   ANN: Yeah? Well, things are different in the real world. I

27   can't wait to see you in ten years. You'll still be the same

28   macho pig with the same macho pig attitude.

29   HENRY: *(Grabbing her again)* I told you to shut that smart

30   mouth.

31   ANN: *(Quietly threatening)* I strongly advise you to get your

32   hands off me.

33   HENRY: I know what you need. You've been begging for this

34   since the beginning of the year. *(He pulls her close to kiss*

35   *her.)*

1   **ANN:** *(Pulling away)* **Hey! That kind of crap might work in**
2   **some tacky tasteless movie, but it won't work with me.**
3   *(He grabs her again.)* **I said to knock it off!** *(She pulls away.)*
4   **Pig!**
5   **HENRY:** **Don't call me names!** *(He slaps her.)*
6   **ANN:** *(She looks at him, straight in the eye.)* **If you ever, ever**
7   **touch me again, the next time you see me will be in court.**
8   **I will have you arrested and press charges so fast, it will**
9   **make your ignorant, macho pig, empty head spin. Don't**
10   **you ever come near me again. Ever!**
11   **HENRY:** **Who's gonna stop me? You? Don't make me laugh.**
12   **ANN:** **This is no joke, Henry. I swear on the heads of my**
13   **future children, if you ever touch me again, I will make**
14   **sure it is taken care of.**
15   **HENRY:** **You gonna get big brother to beat me up?**
16   **ANN:** **No, that would be too easy, and not painful enough. No,**
17   **I will call the police. I will have you arrested. I will go**
18   **in front of a court of law and swear that you handled me**
19   **with violence and assaulted me. I will then sue you and**
20   **your family in civil court for mental and physical stress.**
21   **I will not let go of this. Just know, Henry, that you are**
22   **not dealing with some stupid little girl who thinks you**
23   **are cute. You are dealing with a woman who sees you for**
24   **what you are. A stupid boy who throws a fit when he**
25   **doesn't get his own way.** *(Giving each word importance)* **Now,**
26   **get ... out ... of ... my ... way.**
27   **HENRY:** **Yes, ma'am, Miss District Attorney. You know what**
28   **your real problem is? You just don't like men.**
29   **ANN:** **You're pathetic.**
30   **HENRY:** **Made you think, though, didn't I?**
31   **ANN:** **No, you just reinforced my original thoughts. I love**
32   **men. It's little immature boys I have no time for.**
33   **HENRY:** **Doesn't it seem funny to you that every other girl**
34   **in this school wants to go out with me and you don't?**
35   **Don't you think that's a little strange?**

1 **ANN:** No, it just shows my standards are higher. And face it,
2 Henry, most of the girls you deal with are not exactly on
3 the honor roll.
4 **HENRY:** Yeah ... well ...
5 **ANN:** Good comeback. See ya. *(She turns to walk off.)*
6 **HENRY:** Damn right, you will.
7 **ANN:** *(Turning slowly to look at him)* **Remember what I said, my**
8 **friend. I will make your life a legal hell. Stay away from**
9 **me. Don't talk to me, don't touch me. Pretend I don't exist.**
10 **HENRY:** Maybe I won't have to pretend.
11 **ANN:** That sounds very much like a threat.
12 **HENRY:** Or a promise.
13 **ANN:** You realize, of course, that because of that one statement,
14 I can have a restraining order issued by the courts to
15 keep you away from me?
16 **HENRY:** You cannot.
17 **ANN:** *(She takes a step in towards him.)* **Watch me.**
18 **HENRY:** *(Realizing she is serious, beginning to wonder how*
19 *factual her statements are)* **You're serious? You'd really go**
20 **through all that?**
21 **ANN:** Yes.
22 **HENRY:** You hate me that much?
23 **ANN:** I don't hate you at all. I don't *like* you. But I don't hate
24 you. And I will certainly not allow anyone to manhandle
25 me, or threaten my safety without taking some sort of
26 action.
27 **HENRY:** OK. Fine. I'll leave you alone.
28 **ANN:** If you had simply done that from the beginning, we
29 wouldn't have spent the last ten minutes discussing
30 consequences. Now, I have an honors government class
31 to go to. I assume they await you in auto shop? *(She exits.)*
32 **HENRY:** Jeez, what a bitch.
33 **ANN:** *(From Off-stage)* **I heard that!**
34 **HENRY:** I still have freedom of speech, don't I? *(Quietly)* I do,
35 don't I?

1 # THE LETTER
2
3 **AMY:**   Age 17. Sensitive, warm, friendly, finding out who she is to
4   herself and to the world.
5 **BILL:**   Age 16. Brash, but nice. When he sees a situation that he feels
6   needs to be fixed, he jumps right in. Could be called brutally honest.
7 **ANDREA:**   Very much like Bill, but also considers herself smarter
8   than most kids, which she is. Lacks tact.
9 **SETTING:**   AMY enters, reading a letter. She sits by herself for a
10   moment, sighs deeply, goes back to reading the letter. BILL
11   enters, stops and watches AMY for a moment.
12
13 **BILL:**   So, Amy . . . *(She looks up, tears in her eyes.)* **I see you got**
14   **the letter.**
15 **AMY:**   **Yeah.** *(She holds it up, waving it in front of her.)* **So, is this**
16   **how you really feel?**
17 **BILL:**   **Well, Andrea and I have been talking . . .**
18 **AMY:**   **I'm not talking about Andrea right now. I'm talking**
19   **about you.**
20 **BILL:**   **I know that, Amy. OK, fine. Yes. That is how I feel.**
21 **AMY:**   **I've changed that much over the summer, huh?**
22 **BILL:**   *(Matter of factly)* **I think so.**
23 **ANDREA:**   *(Entering)* **Bill, I think . . .** *(She sees AMY.)* **Oh, you**
24   **gave her the letter, huh?**
25 **AMY:**   **Here it is.**
26 **ANDREA:**   **I want you to know that writing that letter wasn't**
27   **my idea.**
28 **AMY:**   **So you don't agree with all the stuff that's in it?**
29 **ANDREA:**   *(Pausing for a moment)* **I didn't say that.**
30 **AMY:**   **I don't get it. What's wrong with the way I am? How**
31   **come you two are so angry with me?**
32 **ANDREA:**   **We're not angry. We're just . . .**
33 **BILL:**   **Fed up.**
34 **AMY:**   **Fed up? How? What horrible thing have I done to**
35   **either of you?**

1   ANDREA: It's not that you've done anything horrible. You're
2   just . . . different. Right, Bill?
3   BILL: That's a way of putting it. Another way would be to say
4   you've gotten very bitchy . . .
5   AMY: Bitchy?
6   ANDREA: Bitchy is another good way to put it.
7   AMY: What's happening here? I thought you two were
8   supposed to be my best friends.
9   BILL: We are. That's why we're trying to help you.
10   AMY: Help me? By writing this letter and leaving it in my
11   locker? *(She reads from it.)* "Dear Amy, I don't know if any
12   of us want to be your friend anymore . . ." Bill, do you
13   mean to say you're writing this for everyone? For
14   everyone in our group?
15   BILL: We've all talked about it. I guess, yeah, that's what I am
16   saying.
17   ANDREA: Everyone agrees about how much you have
18   changed since last year.
19   AMY: *(She continues reading.)* "You're never there for any of us
20   anymore. When we want to talk to you, you don't seem
21   to listen. You are also becoming very conceited and stuck-
22   up. We hate to tell you this, but you are not as good as
23   you seem to think you are . . ." *(She looks at them.)* What
24   does this all mean?
25   ANDREA: Amy, ever since you went to that drama camp this
26   summer, you walk around like you think you are little
27   Miss Actress. It's stupid. You are so stuck on yourself, it's
28   sickening.
29   AMY: You see it as stuck-up. I see it as being accepted by
30   people who haven't known me since grammar school and
31   seem to think I'm pretty special.
32   BILL: I don't know what those people told you about
33   yourself, but they were wrong. You're just like everyone
34   else, and you better remember that.
35   AMY: No, Bill, I am not like everyone else. I am a special

1   person. An individual. And I know why you're acting like
2   this.
3   ANDREA: It's because we love you. We don't want to have to
4   stop being your friend.
5   AMY: Bull! This is because last week when you were moaning
6   and groaning about Greg for the millionth time, I told
7   you to drop him or drop the subject.
8   ANDREA: See, you recognize it, too, don't you?
9   AMY: All I recognize is the fact that I have been listening to
10   the great saga of you and your boyfriends since second
11   grade. It's old, Andrea, very old.
12   BILL: She's right, Andrea, we're all tired of hearing about it.
13   But Amy . . .
14   AMY: Don't you "But Amy" me, Bill. You're just mad because
15   I won't give you a ride to school anymore.
16   BILL: That's part of it, yes. I think you're being very selfish
17   about it. It's not like it's out of your way, for God's sake.
18   I only live three doors down from you.
19   AMY: Right. But you also start first period. I don't start
20   school until second. Why should I get here an hour earlier
21   just so you don't have to walk?
22   BILL: The Amy we used to know would have.
23   AMY: The Amy you used to know is tired of being the town
24   doormat. *(She looks at both of them.)* You know what the
25   sickening part of this is? Not more than five minutes ago
26   I was crying, thinking what a terrible person I must be
27   for my two best friends to write me such a horrible letter.
28   I thought that maybe I had become selfish and bitchy
29   and *(She refers to the letter)* "inconsiderate of everyone who
30   cares." Well, guess what? I knew this would happen. I
31   didn't want to believe it could, but I knew it would.
32   ANDREA: What do you mean?
33   AMY: When I was at camp this summer, I told my director that
34   for the first time I felt that I had my own personality,
35   that I wasn't just "everyone's friend." I told her I was

1   scared to go back to school because I didn't know if I
2   could keep being the Amy that you all knew or the Amy
3   I had become.
4   BILL: Obviously you made the choice to be the wrong Amy,
5   because the person you've become isn't someone any of
6   us wants as a friend.
7   AMY: She said that might happen. But, you know, I don't
8   care. Either you accept me as I am, because I am growing
9   into a person, not a reflection of my friends, or I can just
10   make new friends.
11 ANDREA: Amy, think about it. Can all of your old friends be
12   wrong?
13 AMY: As a matter of fact, yes, they can. I'm not going to hold
14   my emotions and feelings in while I let you and everyone
15   else use me as a sounding board. If I'm angry, then
16   dammit, I will show it. If I don't want to get to school an
17   hour before I have to just to give your lazy butt a ride,
18   then I won't. If I want to make a choice that doesn't
19   include getting your permission to choose, then that's
20   what I'll do. You know why? Because I am a good person.
21   And if you and everyone else are too narrow to see it,
22   then the hell with you. *(She exits.)*
23 ANDREA: Well . . . I guess she told us.
24 BILL: Like I said, she's become a bitch.
25 ANDREA: Do you think maybe she has a valid point?
26 BILL: No. She's a bitch. If this is who the new Amy is, forget
27   her. I don't need this kind of aggravation in my life.
28 ANDREA: Really. Huh, she'll be back.
29 BILL: I know. I mean, we're her best friends, aren't we?
30 ANDREA: That's right. *(They sit there for a minute. She looks at*
31   *BILL.)*
32 BILL: She'll be back.
33
34
35

HELPING OUT

MARK: A very nice guy; doesn't like to make waves.

ROBB: Also a nice guy, but with little patience for wishy-washy attitudes.

SUZI: Has even less patience than ROBB for wishy-washy ways.

SETTING: Kitchen at MARK's house. A table with a picnic basket and blanket will do.

MARK: *(Preparing a picnic basket, mumbling to himself)* **OK, the sandwiches are made, got the drinks. Oh! The diet coke for Janine.** *(He involuntarily shudders at the thought of forgetting the diet coke. He looks around and can't find any.)* **Oh, no!**

ROBB: *(Entering, watching MARK scurry around looking for the drink)* **Well, this is a pathetic display.**

MARK: *(Surprised)* **Oh, Robb, it's you. You startled me. I thought you might be Janine.**

ROBB: **Please, don't insult me. What are you doing?**

MARK: **Getting the picnic basket ready for today.**

ROBB: **You? Why are you getting it ready?**

MARK: **Janine told . . .** *(Catching himself)* **. . . asked me to.**

ROBB: **Uh-huh.**

MARK: *(Still looking for that diet coke)* **Well, she did. She doesn't have time to do it.**

ROBB: **Uh-huh.**

MARK: **Well, she doesn't!**

ROBB: **I didn't say anything.** *(He reaches around, finds a diet coke, opens it and begins to drink it.)*

MARK: *(At the sound of the can opening, MARK spins around.)* **Is that your diet coke?**

ROBB: **It is now.** *(He drinks.)*

MARK: **Omigod! That's the last one, isn't it.** *(He frantically begins searching for another diet coke.)*

SUZI: *(Entering, sees MARK's frantic search)* **What's he doing?**

1   ROBB: I don't know.
2   MARK: *(Mumbling)* Coke. I need coke.
3   SUZI: *(In an offhand, not serious manner)* He doin' drugs now?
4   MARK: *(To SUZI)* Diet coke, dammit. He drank the last diet
5   coke.
6   SUZI: I'll call the police and phone the newspapers. *(To*
7   *ROBB)* What's his problem?
8   ROBB: Who knows? Did you get the stuff for the picnic?
9   SUZI: Yeah. You want to help me make these sandwiches?
10   ROBB: I'll do it, you did the shopping.
11   SUZI: It's no big deal. I work at the grocery store. Here, you
12   make the sandwiches, I'll cut up some carrots and stuff.
13   *(To MARK)* Oh, Mark, Janine said to pick her up by four.
14   MARK: By four? I thought she didn't get off work until five.
15   SUZI: Nope, she told the manager she wasn't feeling well, so
16   he let her go early.
17   MARK: She's sick?
18   SUZI: Nah, she just didn't feel like staying. She told me that
19   she partied last night after the game and needed to rest
20   up today.
21   MARK: She went home after the game.
22   ROBB: Well, apparently she didn't.
23   MARK: And she left work early?
24   SUZI: Yep.
25   MARK: So, why am I stuck here doing all the work for tonight?
26   ROBB: Well, Mark, probably because you do whatever
27   Janine tells you to. Wouldn't you agree, Suzi?
28   SUZI: Yes, yes, I think that might be the answer, Robb.
29   MARK: She must have some things to take care of.
30   SUZI: Yeah. Like a pretty wicked hangover?
31   MARK: So, while I dropped Janine off at her house, then
32   came home and did nothing, she was . . .
33   ROBB: Over at Josh's party.
34   MARK: You don't know that.
35   SUZI: Yes, we do. We were there, too.

171

1 MARK: I was supposed to go to that party, but Janine said
2   she didn't feel well, so we both went home.
3 ROBB: Well, theoretically, that's true. You went home after
4   you dropped off Janine at her home. You just happened
5   to stay at yours, while Janine went to another home.
6 SUZI: Josh's.
7 MARK: So, while she tells me she can't help with getting the
8   food and stuff together for tonight because she has to
9   work . . .
10 SUZI: With me, remember, at a grocery store where there is
11   food . . .
12 ROBB: That Suzi so kindly bought, brought over and now we,
13   together as a couple, are making into our dinner for the
14   evening . . .
15 MARK: And she leaves that job early so she can rest . . .
16 SUZI: Nurse a hangover is more like it . . .
17 ROBB: That neither Suzi or I have, because we don't party
18   like some people . . .
19 SUZI: Some people who have no respect for themselves or
20   others . . .
21 ROBB: Who lie to certain other people . . .
22 SUZI: Certain other people that are making picnic dinners
23   for liars . . .
24 MARK: And I am panicking because Robb drank the last diet
25   coke in the house and Janine won't drink anything other
26   than that . . .
27 SUZI: Oh, I'd say she drank something other than that last
28   night, wouldn't you, Robb?
29 ROBB: Not that I was counting, but she drank quite a few
30   coolers . . .
31 SUZI: Five . . .
32 ROBB: Seven . . . but who's counting, right?
33 SUZI: Right . . .
34 MARK: She told me she wanted to go home. I went home. I
35   *wanted* to go to Josh's party.

1   ROBB: But Janine told you to go home . . .
2   MARK: Yeah. Hey . . . wait a minute.
3   SUZI: Yes?
4   MARK: Why am I here, doing the picnic stuff, tearing the
5   room apart looking for her damn diet coke, staying at
6   home while she parties, making her stupid turkey
7   sandwich with non-fat mayonnaise because she's at work
8   and really isn't at work? This sucks!
9   ROBB: Hello? We've only been telling you this for the last
10   five months, haven't we?
11   SUZI: I think so. Yes, yes, it was definitely us.
12   MARK: So, now what do I do?
13   SUZI: You call that wench and tell her to make her own damn
14   sandwich and that you're breaking up with her.
15   MARK: Breaking up?
16   ROBB: Yes, breaking up. For God's sake, Mark, you've
17   become the school joke.
18   MARK: I have?
19   SUZI: It's embarrassing. Everyone knows how she treats
20   you, and you just ignore it.
21   MARK: She treats me OK.
22   SUZI: She treats you like dirt.
23   ROBB: If Suzi treated me the way Janine treats you, no way
24   would I put up with it.
25   SUZI: She walks all over you, lies to you, tells you what to
26   do. And the sickening thing is, you seem to like it.
27   MARK: I don't like the way she treats me. But it's not always
28   like this. Some times are really good between us. You're
29   not with us when we're alone.
30   SUZI: Spare me the intimate details.
31   ROBB: *(Leaning in)* I'll listen.
32   MARK: No, that's not what I mean. Get your mind out of the
33   gutter.
34   SUZI: *(Smacking ROBB)* Pig.
35   ROBB: Sorry.

1   MARK: When we're alone, we laugh and talk, and I feel like
2   she really listens and likes me.
3   SUZI: Mark, she uses you. I didn't want to tell you this, but
4   she was *laughing* and *talking* last night with Steve.
5   MARK: She was? With Steve?
6   ROBB: Yeah.
7   SUZI: *(Handing him the phone)* Call her, Mark. Tell her that
8   you've had enough.
9   MARK: *(Taking the phone)* Call her?
10   ROBB: Come on, Mark. Are you going to be her doormat for
11   life?
12   MARK: But . . .
13   SUZI: She was doing more than just *laughing* and *talking*
14   with Steve.
15   MARK: You're right. Look at this. I spent the day making all
16   this food she likes and nothing I like. I *hate* fat-free
17   mayonnaise. I don't drink diet coke. I drink root beer.
18   But she doesn't, so I get diet coke. She wants me to go
19   home last night, so I go. What am I, her dog? Her personal
20   pet? Her slave? I don't need this!
21   ROBB: Damn right you don't.
22   SUZI: You deserve better.
23   MARK: Damn right I deserve better. *(Dialing the phone)*
24   I'm calling her right now. This is it. It's over. I don't need
25   this. Hello . . . Janine? Hi, Mark . . . Listen, I need to talk
26   to you . . . Yes, I got the fat-free stuff, but I . . . uh-huh.
27   Yes, Suzi told me you left work early. That's what I
28   wanted to talk to you about . . . uh-huh . . . I see . . . Good,
29   I'm glad you're feeling better . . . but I. . . . oh, really? I
30   didn't know that . . . But the point I want to make
31   is . . . huh? No, Robb drank the last diet coke . . . *(He looks*
32   *over to ROBB, who toasts him with the can.)* Well, why couldn't
33   you have gotten some while you were at work? . . . I see.
34   Well, I can understand that . . . Wait a minute. I was
35   talking about . . . Oh, you did, huh? Josh's party? . . .

1   Steve? Yes, I know Steve, of course I know Steve . . . Robb
2   and Suzi . . . Yes, they're here. They said that . . . That's
3   what I . . . He did? . . . He was? . . . No, I didn't know
4   that . . . Oh, wow . . . You're kidding . . . No, I totally
5   understand. You had no choice . . . Yeah, I'll see you in a
6   little bit . . . Me, too. Oh, what'd I call for? Uh, to ask you
7   to bring some diet coke from home, 'cause I'm out . . . Oh,
8   OK, no problem. Sure. OK, see you in about an hour.
9   ROBB: *(In disgust)* Boy, you told her, huh?
10   SUZI: *(Sarcastic)* I bet she's burning from that tongue lashing
11   you gave her. I know if Robb ever talked to me like that,
12   I'd be reduced to tears. Please, Robb, don't ever speak to
13   me so cruelly.
14   ROBB: Well, at least she's bringing her own diet coke.
15   MARK: No, I told her I'd swing by the store and pick up a
16   six-pack.
17   SUZI: Oh, for God's sake, Mark, you're pathetic. Strap on a
18   backbone.
19   ROBB: I can't believe you. After what we told you about her
20   and Steve.
21   MARK: She explained that.
22   SUZI: I bet she did.
23   MARK: She said that Steve was having some problems at
24   home so she was just trying to make him forget and put
25   him in a better mood.
26   SUZI: Oh, that's what they're calling it these days?
27   MARK: Shut up, Suzi.
28   SUZI: What a pitiful display. Look at you, all forgiving, ready
29   to crawl back . . .
30   MARK: There's nothing to forgive.
31   ROBB: Come on, man, she sent you home so she could go to
32   Josh's party and *party.*
33   MARK: She said that she was reading a book, getting ready
34   for bed when Steve called her. He asked her to come so
35   he could talk about some things.

1   SUZI: What things?!
2   MARK: Janine said it was private, that she couldn't betray
3   his confidence.
4   SUZI: Oh, my God. And you believe her?
5   MARK: What else do you expect me to do?
6   ROBB: Get some self-respect and tell her good-bye.
7   MARK: I don't want to. Understand? I do not want to. How
8   much clearer can I make it?
9   SUZI: So, you're just going to be miserable?
10   MARK: I wasn't miserable until you two got here and started
11   getting me all worked up over, what it turns out, is
12   nothing. As a matter of fact, Janine and I get along pretty
13   well on our own. We only fight when you two have put
14   something in my mind.
15   ROBB: Oh, so we're the evil ones, huh? We conjure up some
16   little spell to make you see how she really is . . .
17   SUZI: Bubble bubble, toil and trouble . . . which is what
18   you're in for if you stay with Janine much longer.
19   MARK: You know, I think that is my problem, if it is a problem.
20   And I don't think it is. Janine and I are fine, when you
21   two aren't around.
22   SUZI: It's pretty obvious you can't tell who your real friends
23   are, Mark.
24   MARK: Maybe, but I know who I need to be with right now,
25   and it isn't you two. *(He picks up his basket of food and the*
26   *blanket for the picnic.)* You know the way out. *(He heads out,*
27   *then stops.)* And maybe we better not sit with you two
28   tonight. I think Janine and I need to be alone. *(He exits.)*
29   SUZI: Well.
30   ROBB: I guess he told us.
31   SUZI: Hey, it's his problem. Let him deal with it.
32   ROBB: Well, we're not mopping up this mess when he comes
33   crying back to us because she left him like a used Kleenex.
34   SUZI: Yes, we will. We always do. Sometimes we're just as
35   pitiful as he is. Come on, let's go.

1   **ROBB:**   Who are we going to sit with tonight?

2   **SUZI:**   Each other. Charlie and Jessica said they weren't

3   going and Jeff and Angela are mad at us about something.

4   I don't know what their problem is.

5   **ROBB:**   Ever since we told Angela that we saw Jeff with

6   another girl when she was out of town, they're all mad

7   at us.

8   **SUZI:**   How were we supposed to know that cute little blond

9   was his cousin?

10   **ROBB:**   They got all mad at us just because we tried to help.

11   **SUZI:**   Go figure. What's wrong with some people?

12   **ROBB:**   Really! You try and be a friend.

13   **SUZI:**   Some people just don't appreciate us.

14   **ROBB:**   Their loss.

15   **SUZI:**   That's right.

16   **ROBB:**   So, who do you want to hang out with tonight?

17   **SUZI:**   I don't know. Each other? *(They look at each other and*

18   *shrug. Exit)*

19

20

21

22

23

24

25

26

27

28

29

30

31

32

33

34

35

1 # A GATHERING OF FRIENDS
2
3 *The partners:*
4   ***KAY and RICK:*** Fantasize about love, seldom argue, still in
5   the hand-holding stage.
6   ***BILL and MARY:*** Short-tempered, frustrated that things are
7   not perfect, but blame one another for the problems.
8   ***KRIS and JOHN:*** Been together the longest, know each other
9   inside and out, great and deep love, but know each other's weak
10   spots and have no problem digging into them.
11 *The place:*
12   The first scene takes place at KRIS's house. The second two take
13   place each in their own spots, one Down Right, one Down Left,
14   and then move into the area of KRIS's house which is Center
15   Stage. The couples have the place to themselves for the evening.
16   The women have planned a dinner party; the guys do guy things.
17
18 JOHN: *(A bit surly)* **Where do you want this?** *(He is holding a*
19   *dish of dip or something.)*
20 KRIS: *(Just as surly back to him)* **I told you earlier, I want**
21   **everything that is finger food over on that table. The rest**
22   **of it goes over here by the dining table.**
23 JOHN: **If I had heard you, you think I would have asked?**
24 KRIS: **If you listened, maybe you wouldn't have to ask.**
25 JOHN: **Maybe if you said something worth listening to, I**
26   **would listen more often.**
27 KRIS: **We're are not going to get into this argument tonight,**
28   **do you understand?**
29 JOHN: **Don't tell me about arguing. I am simply making a**
30   **statement ...**
31 KRIS: **You are making a fight ...**
32 JOHN: **You're the one that wants to fight.**
33 KRIS: **I am sick of this discussion.**
34 JOHN: **Then shut up ...** *(He leaves the scene and goes into the*
35   *kitchen.)*

1   **KRIS:**   Don't tell me to shut up ... *(She follows him into the*
2   *kitchen, talking.)*
3   **MARY:**   *(In their own area Down Left)* **Bill, are you sure you want**
4   **to go tonight?**
5   **BILL:**   I told you yes.
6   **MARY:**   You haven't been acting very enthusiastic about it.
7   **BILL:**   Well, what do you want me to do? Jump up and down?
8   **Sing and dance?**
9   **MARY:**   No, Bill, I just want you to be nice.
10   **BILL:**   I'm nice to everyone, Mary.
11   **MARY:**   Yes, everyone but me.
12   **BILL:**   Here we go again.
13   **MARY:**   We are not going anywhere again. I just said ...
14   **BILL:**   That I am nice to everyone except you.
15   **MARY:**   Well, it's true.
16   **BILL:**   So what? You want to break up?
17   **MARY:**   I never said that.
18   **BILL:**   No, but it's what you want, isn't it?
19   **MARY:**   No, it's not what I want.
20   **BILL:**   Hey, if you want out of this relationship, say so. I never
21   thought it would last anyway.
22   **MARY:**   Here we go again. Poor little Bill. Everyone always
23   leaves him.
24   **BILL:**   It's true.
25   **MARY:**   Oh, please, I refuse to have this discussion.
26   **BILL:**   So, do you still want to go?
27   **MARY:**   Kris and John are waiting for us, so yes, let's go.
28   **BILL:**   Fine, I'll go. It won't be fun, but I will go.
29   **MARY:**   Great. Swell. Another terrific evening of merriment
30   lies before us. *(They exit.)*
31   **KRIS:**   *(From Off-stage)* **John, could you peel the carrots,**
32   **please?**
33   **JOHN:**   *(Also from Off-stage)* **No.**
34   **KRIS:**   *(Still from Off-stage)* **Jerk.**
35   **KAY:**   *(In the area Down Right)* **Rick, are you almost ready?**

1   **RICK:**   Yeah. *(He enters.)* **You look great.**

2   **KAY:**   So do you.

3   **RICK:**   I am so lucky to have you.

4   **KAY:**   I'm the lucky one.

5   **RICK:**   *(Handing her a small package)* **Happy anniversary.**

6   **KAY:**   *(Handing him one, too)* **Happy anniversary to you.** *(They*

7   *both open their gifts. Hers is a "Big Hunk" candy bar.)* **Oh, a**

8   **"Big Hunk" from my big hunk.**

9   **RICK:**   *(He opens his.)* **Strawberry flavored Chapstick?**

10   **KAY:**   It's the kind I always use, so even when I'm not around,

11   you can still taste my lips on yours.

12   **RICK:**   *(Hugging her)* **I want you to always be around.**

13   **KAY:**   You can count on it. Just think, we've been together for

14   a whole month.

15   **RICK:**   And they said it wouldn't last.

16   **KAY:**   Listen, do you want to get together with Kris and John,

17   and Bill and Mary tonight?

18   **RICK:**   We said we'd be there. You know how Kris gets if

19   anyone changes plans.

20   **KAY:**   True. And besides, her parents are gone. We will be

21   alone!

22   **RICK:**   Alone with those other people. How long do you think

23   we will be there before the arguments begin?

24   **KAY:**   The minute they walk in the door, they will be at it.

25   **RICK:**   I'm not looking forward to it, that's for sure.

26   **KAY:**   Right after dinner, we're out of there, OK?

27   **RICK:**   No argument here.

28   **KAY:**   Then let's go. The sooner we get there, the faster we

29   can leave and be alone! *(They exit.)*

30   **KRIS:**   *(Entering the center area, MARY follows.)* **I don't know**

31   about you, but I am not looking forward to witnessing

32   the great romance tonight, are you?

33   **MARY:**   You mean Kay and Rick? Gag me. If she calls him

34   "Big Hunk" tonight, I will puke on her feet.

35   **KRIS:**   Can you believe them? Makes my skin crawl. Hey,

1   what's with Bill tonight?
2 MARY: I was going to ask you the same thing about John.
3 KRIS: He's in a mood. I'm ignoring it.
4 MARY: So's Bill. I don't know how you do it. You just go on as
5   if it's nothing.
6 KRIS: That's your problem right there. Their moods are
7   nothing. God, they talk about women and PMS. Men are
8   worse. At least with women it's only once a month. With
9   men it's year round.
10 MARY: *(Laughing)* No kidding. *(BILL enters.)*
11 BILL: What's so funny?
12 MARY: Nothing. *(She and KRIS look at each other and burst out*
13   *laughing, exiting the area.)*
14 BILL: Women, can't live with them, can't live without them ...
15 JOHN and BILL: But let's give it a shot.
16 BILL: When are Rick and Kay getting here?
17 JOHN: I don't know. Rick said they'd be here about seven.
18   It's seven-thirty now. *(Calling)* Kris, I'm getting hungry.
19 KRIS: *(From Off-stage)* If you had peeled those carrots you
20   could have had them with some dip. Oh, well.
21 JOHN: Great. Whatever happened to the woman serving the
22   man?
23 MARY: *(Entering with a bag of chips and a can of dip)* Here, your
24   majesty. Live it up. *(She exits.)*
25 BILL: Another swell evening, huh? Let's just hope Rick and
26   Kay aren't their usual sickening selves.
27 JOHN: *(Mimicking)* Oh, Kay, you're the best thing that ever
28   happened to me.
29 BILL: *(Mimicking)* No, Rick, you're the best thing that ever
30   happened to me.
31 JOHN: *(Embracing BILL)* No, Kay, you are.
32 BILL: *(Embracing JOHN)* No, Ricky, it's you. *(KRIS and MARY*
33   *enter on this.)*
34 KRIS: Well, it's finally come to this.
35 MARY: I knew we were seeing too much of each other but,

1   John, Bill, I didn't realize how close you two had become.

2   JOHN: No, no. I'm Rick.

3   BILL: And I'm Kay. *(They hug and act sickening.)*

4   KRIS: Looks right to me.

5   MARY: Do you think we will be able to get through the

6   evening without an insulin injection?

7   KRIS: Unlikely. God, don't those two irritate you?

8   BILL: They'll get over it when they've been together as long

9   as we have.

10   MARY: What are you talking about? You never treated me

11   like that.

12   BILL: I did too.

13   JOHN: I didn't.

14   KRIS: No kidding. What you see now is what it has always

15   been.

16   JOHN: You act like it's a bad thing.

17   KRIS: Just once I'd like you to tell me I look nice.

18   JOHN: I do.

19   KRIS: When? Name the time.

20   JOHN: I can't remember offhand. *(There is a knock at the door.)*

21   I can't have this discussion now because I have to answer

22   the door.

23   KRIS: Lucky for you, huh?

24   KAY: Hi, everyone. Who's lucky? Me? I know. *(She looks at*

25   *RICK adoringly, who looks back at her likewise.)*

26   RICK: I'm the lucky one.

27   MARY: I have to go get something from the kitchen.

28   BILL: What?

29   MARY: I don't know, I just have to get it.

30   KRIS: I'll help you. *(They exit.)*

31   RICK: *(Sitting, pulling KAY on his lap)* So, what's going on, guys?

32   BILL: Not much. *(He and JOHN exchange looks while KAY and*

33   *RICK hug.)*

34   JOHN: *(Calling out)* Kris, you need any help in there?

35   KRIS: *(Calling back)* Nope, you stay and entertain our guests.

1   **JOHN:** *(Under his breath)* **Great.**

2   **BILL:** **So, Rick, what's new?**

3   **KAY:** **It's our anniversary. Sweetie pie, do you mind if I go**

4   **into the kitchen? I'll just be gone for a minute. I want to**

5   **show the girls what you got me.**

6   **RICK:** **OK, but hurry back.**

7   **KAY:** **I will.** *(She kisses him on the nose.)*

8   **BILL:** **You got her a gift?**

9   **RICK:** **Just a candy bar. One month. What the heck, huh?**

10   **Isn't she great?**

11   **JOHN:** *(No enthusiasm)* **Swell.**

12   **BILL:** *(Same)* **Terrific.**

13   **RICK:** *(Looking adoringly off in her direction)* **Yeah.**

14   **BILL:** **Hey, I got those brochures from the travel agent about**

15   **the Washington trip. You want to see them?**

16   **RICK:** **Oh, yeah.**

17   **JOHN:** **You're still on for it, aren't you?**

18   **RICK:** **Wouldn't miss it.**

19   **JOHN:** **You better not. It's too late to get someone to take**

20   **your place.**

21   **BILL:** **I can't wait. On a motorcycle up the coast to Washing-**

22   **ton. Here, take a look.** *(The guys become engrossed in their*

23   *private discussion, not noticing the women have re-entered.)*

24   **KRIS:** **Mary, put that dish over here. Kay, can you get the**

25   **candles and put them in the silver holders?**

26   **KAY:** **This is so romantic. The three of us couples having**

27   **dinner by candlelight.**

28   **MARY:** **No parents.**

29   **KAY:** **Ooohhh! You know what I should do? Cut up the "Big**

30   **Hunk" and serve it for dessert. Wouldn't that be romantic?**

31   **KRIS:** **Oh, yeah. Nothing more romantic than scraping taffy**

32   **off your teeth with your thumbnail.**

33   **MARY:** **Let's not, OK?**

34   **KAY:** **Look at them over there. Aren't they adorable? Sitting**

35   **like real men and discussing real man stuff. Look at the**

1   shoulders on my Ricky.
2   MARY: Look at the belly on my Bill.
3   KRIS: You are so mean, Mary.
4   MARY: *(Laughing)* Yeah, I know.
5   KAY: You are, Mary. You say mean things to Bill. You do to
6   John, too, Kris.
7   MARY: Oh, brother.
8   KRIS: Spare us your insight of one month long love, OK?
9   KAY: Maybe that's your problem. You two have just become
10   too complacent. You've lost the spark for keeping love
11   alive. It's little things that make it last.
12   KRIS: Oh, yeah. I know that if John gave me a candy bar I
13   would just swoon at the romance of it.
14   KAY: It's the thought that counts. We think of each other
15   before ourselves.
16   KRIS: Great. Happy for you. Can we eat now?
17   KAY: I'm just saying . . .
18   MARY: *(Calling to the guys)* Dinner's ready.
19   BILL: We'll be there in a second.
20   KRIS: What's so interesting?
21   JOHN: Bill got these brochures about Washington and Oregon.
22   MARY: When are you guys planning on leaving?
23   BILL: The Friday before spring break.
24   KRIS: So you'll be gone the whole week?
25   JOHN: Yeah. Fishing, camping, motorcycling.
26   BILL: Man stuff.
27   RICK: I have been looking forward to this since our freshman
28   year.
29   BILL: It's going to be great.
30   KAY: What are you talking about?
31   RICK: Our trip up the coast.
32   KAY: Rick, honey, my parents wouldn't let me go on a trip
33   like that. Especially on a motorcycle.
34   KRIS: That works out well, because the women aren't going.
35   KAY: What?

1	RICK:	Kay, it's just me, Bill, and John.
2	KAY:	You're going to be gone the whole week?
3	RICK:	Yes ... is it OK?
4	JOHN:	*(To KRIS, quietly)* He's asking permission?
5	KRIS:	But that will be the time of our two-month anniversary.
6	RICK:	We can celebrate it when I get back.
7	KAY:	It won't be the same.
8	RICK:	I'll make up for it.
9	KRIS:	Kay, you've known about the guys planning this trip
10		for years.
11	KAY:	That was before Rick and I started going out. I didn't
12		think he'd still want to go if he had a girlfriend.
13	JOHN:	I have a girlfriend, and I want to go.
14	KRIS:	Hell, I want him to. I need a break.
15	MARY:	Tell me about it. Besides, it will be fun. Kris and I
16		have already planned to hit every mall within a sixty-mile
17		radius. You've known about that, too. You were coming
18		with us.
19	KAY:	But that was before I had a boyfriend.
20	MARY:	You mean you don't want to go?
21	KAY:	I'd rather be with Rick.
22	RICK:	Honey, I'd like to be with you, too. But the guys. I can't
23		let them down.
24	KAY:	Oh, I see. But you can let me down, is that it?
25	BILL:	Uh-oh, trouble in paradise.
26	KAY:	There is no trouble, because there isn't a paradise.
27	RICK:	What does that mean?
28	KAY:	I guess I was wrong about you. You aren't the
29		considerate man I thought you were. You're just like
30		these adolescents.
31	JOHN:	Excuse me? What the hell does that mean?
32	KAY:	You three. Off to do your big macho thing.
33	KRIS:	Kay, they have been planning this for years.
34	KAY:	Well, Rick, you can just unplan it.
35	BILL:	Oh, no he can't.

1   MARY: Kay, you're being unreasonable.
2   KRIS: Really. It's not like he's moving to another state.
3   KAY: He may as well be.
4   RICK: Come on, Kay. This is stupid.
5   KAY: Don't you dare call me stupid!
6   RICK: I didn't say you were. I said your actions were.
7   JOHN: Oh, boy. A fight.
8   KAY: Shut up, John.
9   KRIS: Don't tell my boyfriend to shut up.
10 KAY: You all shut up. This is between me and Rick.
11 BILL: No, it's between all of us because we are all affected. I
12   want to know right now if Rick is going with us or being
13   woman whipped into staying.
14 RICK: I am going. I said I was going when I was fourteen.
15   Now that I'm eighteen, I am certainly not changing my
16   mind.
17 KAY: So, in other words, you still have the mind of a fourteen-
18   year-old.
19 RICK: No, but you sure are acting like one.
20 KRIS: I think we all need to settle down now. This is getting out
21   of hand.
22 KAY: No. It's all coming into focus. Obviously Rick's friends
23   mean more to him than I do.
24 MARY: You're just being selfish, Kay.
25 KAY: Selfish? Look at those three males. They are the epitome
26   of selfishness. Have they offered to help once? No, they
27   expect the women to serve them. They plan their little
28   excursions into the wilderness while we, the women, are
29   supposed to wait patiently for their return. Think again.
30 JOHN: Hey, I think you've said enough.
31 KAY: I haven't even begun.
32 JOHN: Listen, Kay. I have heard enough. I don't know what
33   your problem is, but knock it off. This is supposed to be a
34   nice dinner with friends.
35 KAY: *(Scoffing at the word)* Friends. Some friends. You two plan

1   to take my boyfriend away for a week and you two are

2   encouraging this.

3   **KRIS:** Kay, sometimes men need to be alone.

4   **MARY:** Hell, so do women.

5   **KAY:** That's because you two have let the love slip away from

6   your lives. *(Turning to RICK)* And now it's happening to us.

7   **RICK:** No, it's not. If you don't want me to go, I won't.

8   **KAY:** *(Smiling through her tears)* Really?

9   **BILL:** *(Unbelieving)* Really?

10   **JOHN:** Oh, God.

11   **MARY:** Oh, no.

12   **KRIS:** Kay ...

13   **RICK:** Hey, if she doesn't want me to go, I won't go.

14   **KAY:** You really wouldn't go?

15   **RICK:** Does it mean that much to you?

16   **KRIS:** Say it doesn't, Kay. John and I need a break from each

17   other.

18   **MARY:** Hear, hear.

19   **KAY:** Well ...

20   **RICK:** Whatever you want is what I will do.

21   **KAY:** Then go. Have a good time.

22   **KRIS:** Hallelujah!

23   **BILL:** *(High-fives MARY.)* We're still on.

24   **JOHN:** Maybe I don't want to go now.

25   **KRIS:** What!

26   **JOHN:** Maybe I don't like this wishy-washy attitude from

27   Rick.

28   **KRIS:** Oh, jeez.

29   **JOHN:** I don't like it.

30   **BILL:** Come one, John. It's set, let's just make the plans,

31   OK?

32   **JOHN:** I don't know.

33   **KAY:** I said it was all right, John. It really is.

34   **JOHN:** I don't need your permission, Kay.

35   **KAY:** I didn't say you did. I just said ...

1 JOHN: I don't like your coming in here and causing problems.
2 RICK: Just a minute, John . . .
3 JOHN: Hey, I need to have my say.
4 KRIS: No, John, you really don't . . .
5 JOHN: Don't start acting like Kay, Kris.
6 BILL and MARY: Uh-oh . . .
7 JOHN: Just remember your place.
8 KRIS: My place. What the hell does that mean . . . my place?
9 JOHN: That there are some things you shouldn't interfere
10   in . . .
11 KAY: Don't tell her how to act.
12 JOHN: I'm telling you the same thing.
13 KAY: Don't tell me what to do, either.
14 KRIS: I'll say what I want in my own home and anywhere
15   else for that matter.
16 MARY: Maybe we all better sit down and eat.
17 KAY: Maybe we all just better leave.
18 JOHN: Maybe you should.
19 KAY: Maybe we will. Come on, Rick. *(She exits.)*
20 RICK: I'll call you guys later and we'll talk about the trip.
21 JOHN: If she allows you to use the phone, give us a ring.
22 KAY: *(Calling from Off-stage)* Rick, come on!
23 RICK: See you. *(He exits.)*
24 JOHN: Wuss. Come on, Kris, I'll help you in the kitchen.
25 KRIS: OK. *(She and MARY exchange looks that speak volumes.)*
26 MARY: Well, this was a great evening.
27 BILL: John has a point, you know.
28 MARY: Uh-huh.
29 BILL: Well, he does . . . kind of. Kris shouldn't have stepped
30   in. It wasn't her argument.
31 MARY: I guess not. Boy, can you believe Kay and Rick? *(KRIS*
32   *and JOHN appear Down Left.)*
33 KRIS: Can you believe Kay and Rick? *(KAY and RICK appear*
34   *Down Right.)*
35 KAY: Can you believe John and Kris? Not to mention Bill

1   and Mary.
2   KRIS: He sure has her tied up, huh?
3   JOHN: No kidding.
4   MARY: She sure has him tied up, huh?
5   BILL: No kidding.
6   KAY: Those guys have some serious problems.
7   RICK: No kidding.
8   KRIS, BILL and KAY: I give them another month before they
9   break up.
10 MARY, JOHN and RICK: Less.
11 MARY, KRIS and KAY: It's too bad they aren't as happy as we
12   are.
13 BILL, RICK and JOHN: They just don't know what it takes.
14
15
16
17
18
19
20
21
22
23
24
25
26
27
28
29
30
31
32
33
34
35

Photo by Kris Alana.

Mary Krell-Oishi
and her husband Harris

About the Author

Mary Krell-Oishi has just begun her third decade teaching Theater at Sunny Hills High School in Fullerton, California. (She began teaching at the age of nine years old ... honest!) She was named Playwright of the Year by the California State Thespians in 1995. Mary continues to be inspired and enriched by the students who have passed through her classroom and crossed the stage.

Mary takes an enormous amount of pride and joy from the many letters and e-mails she has received from young actors from as far away as Ireland and New Zealand who have performed her short plays and have wanted to share their excitement with her. She plans to continue to write for young adults for both the stage and in fiction.

Married since 1977 to her wonderful husband, Harris, she splits her living time between Yorba Linda and Big Bear, California. As her son, Rick, is soon to be married to the lovely Shay, Mary cannot wait to have grandchildren to take to the theater, shower with gifts, spoil and send back to the unsuspecting parents.

Also by Mary Krell-Oishi:

Scenes That Happen

Scenes Keep Happening

Perspectives

See order forms in back of book.

NOTES

Order Form

Meriwether Publishing Ltd.
PO Box 7710
Colorado Springs, CO 80933-7710
Phone: 800-937-5297 Fax: 719-594-9916
Website: www.meriwether.com

Please send me the following books:

More Scenes That Happen #BK-B112	**$15.95**
by Mary Krell-Oishi	
More real-life snapshots of teen lives	
Scenes That Happen #BK-B156	**$15.95**
by Mary Krell-Oishi	
Dramatized snapshots of high school life	
Scenes Keep Happening #BK-B280	**$15.95**
by Mary Krell-Oishi	
More real-life snapshots of teen lives	
Perspectives #BK-B206	**$14.95**
Mary Krell-Oishi	
Relevant scenes for teens	
Winning Monologs for Young Actors #BK-B127	**$15.95**
by Peg Kehret	
Honest-to-life monologs for young actors	
Encore! More Winning Monologs for Young Actors #BK-B144	**$15.95**
by Peg Kehret	
More honest-to-life monologs for young actors	
The Flip Side #BK-B221	**$15.95**
by Heather H. Henderson	
64 point-of-view monologs for teens	

These and other fine Meriwether Publishing books are available at your local bookstore or direct from the publisher. Prices subject to change without notice. Check our website or call for current prices.

Name: _____ e-mail: _____

Organization name: _____

Address: _____

City: _____ State: _____

Zip: _____ Phone: _____

❑ **Check enclosed**

❑ **Visa / MasterCard / Discover #** _____

Signature: _____   Expiration date: _____ / _____
  (required for credit card orders)

Colorado residents: Please add 3% sales tax.
Shipping: Include $3.95 for the first book and 75¢ for each additional book ordered.

❑ *Please send me a copy of your complete catalog of books and plays.*

Order Form

Meriwether Publishing Ltd.
PO Box 7710
Colorado Springs, CO 80933-7710
Phone: 800-937-5297 Fax: 719-594-9916
Website: www.meriwether.com

Please send me the following books:

_____ **More Scenes That Happen #BK-B112** $15.95
by Mary Krell-Oishi
More real-life snapshots of teen lives

_____ **Scenes That Happen #BK-B156** $15.95
by Mary Krell-Oishi
Dramatized snapshots of high school life

_____ **Scenes Keep Happening #BK-B280** $15.95
by Mary Krell-Oishi
More real-life snapshots of teen lives

_____ **Perspectives #BK-B206** $14.95
Mary Krell-Oishi
Relevant scenes for teens

_____ **Winning Monologs for Young Actors** $15.95
#BK-B127
by Peg Kehret
Honest-to-life monologs for young actors

_____ **Encore! More Winning Monologs for** $15.95
Young Actors #BK-B144
by Peg Kehret
More honest-to-life monologs for young actors

_____ **The Flip Side #BK-B221** $15.95
by Heather H. Henderson
64 point-of-view monologs for teens

These and other fine Meriwether Publishing books are available at
your local bookstore or direct from the publisher. Prices subject to
change without notice. Check our website or call for current prices.

Name: _____ e-mail: _____

Organization name: _____

Address: _____

City: _____ State: _____

Zip: _____ Phone: _____

❑ **Check enclosed**
❑ **Visa / MasterCard / Discover #** _____

Signature: _____   *Expiration date:* _____ / _____
     (required for credit card orders)

Colorado residents: Please add 3% sales tax.
Shipping: Include $3.95 for the first book and 75¢ for each additional book ordered.

❑ *Please send me a copy of your complete catalog of books and plays.*